MW01087217

Book Endorsements

Radical Mindfulness

"Simply masterful! Truly one of the most profoundly simple and engaging books I have ever read. A powerful journey to the core of what it is to be human. That, as Daniel Gutierrez so powerfully points out, the instructions for your life are within you."

—TERESA DE GROSBOIS, #1 International Bestselling Author of *Mass Influence*, Founder & Chair of the Evolutionary Business Council

"*Radical Mindfulness* is a powerful and inspiring book. Daniel has become vulnerable and sagacious at the same time. This book is one of those books, which can change your life. Thanks for sharing your wisdom I know your Mom is proud."

—CYNTHIA M RUIZ, Author, Professor & Inspirational Speaker

"Once I started, I couldn't stop. I love the journey, the fact I could visualize your experience through your descriptions. The book is wonderful and full of truth which is what we all seek. The exercises for radical mindfulness are easy to work with. Breathing always works. Thank you for the honor and pleasure to read it before the printed matter. The book is an easy and adventuresome read that enhances the reader's life with travel and requires little search for the clarity in the message. Feeling good and connected to source is the ultimate way of life. When we can go there, life kicks into an amazing flow of appreciation and gratitude."

—LYDIA COLÓN PERERA QUILLA, Villa Mountain Retreat Center, Peru

"We need spiritual leaders, beyond religions and more, spiritual leaders who are what they say. Daniel is exactly what he says, what he shares. Calm. Kind. Happy. He shares his spiritual experience, directly to our soul. His book is a treasure of Humility and simplicity. So simple, so profound, so adapted to our world."

—**MICHEL PASCAL**, Meditation Teacher, & Singer

"Daniel's book radically proves that the power of a mother instills a spirit within all of us that we should always cherish; specifically, in this book Daniel highlights the power and belief that his mother provided him is a road map for his new journey with clear mindfulness for genuine success."

—**FRANK CARBAJAL**, Co-Author of *Building the Latino Future
"Success Stories for the Next Generation"* &
Co-Author of *El Futuro Latino*

"In Daniel's life-changing book he takes us on amazing journeys as he preaches as a youth in his impoverished Texas town and hobnobs as a young entrepreneur with the rich and famous in the plush clubs of Manhattan; as he meets with his spirit animal in the oldest living Inca city in Peru and performs a blessing ceremony at the holy beside of his dying mother. But perhaps the most exciting journey is the one he leads us on away from the pain of our past, to the realm of unbounded peace and silence through applying his powerful Radical Mindfulness techniques."

—**DEBRA PONEMAN**, Bestselling Author &
Founder of *Yes to Success* Seminars

"In a world of distractions that constantly challenge our wellbeing, it's invaluable to have a quick guide that helps us become present to our life NOW so we can focus on fulfilling the reason we're here. As one who has led both spiritual awakening trips through the jungles of Peru and corporate events for anxiety-ridden cubicle-dwellers, Daniel Gutierrez is uniquely qualified to bring peace to the chaos of the modern psyche and teach us how to come from our heart to have the most satisfying life possible."

—**SCOTT WARE**, Publisher of *Radiance Magazine*

"Daniel brings his readers on a powerful journey of radical transformation from the illusion of pain to the rich rewards of reality. Read this book, join Daniel on this journey, and find the joy and meaning you are seeking for yourself!"

—**CAMILLE LEON,** Founder of
The Holistic Chamber of Commerce

"As a student and practitioner in the healing arts, understanding mindfulness can be an overwhelming thought as we live & learn from our healing journeys. *Radical Mindfulness* is a must read and will be my go-to for many years to come. The simplicity of how Daniel expresses his words in a manner that both a novice or expert can comprehend is a real piece of art. His raw, honest, and emotional style of writing captivated my brain to get REAL PRESENT and ask myself what I was feeling right at this exact moment in time. Something that is not an easy practice to do. *Radical Mindfulness* is a brilliant piece of work!"

—**MELISSA JOY BOTTEN,** CHN, RYT, CAM,
Healing in Heels Preventative Medicine

"To say a man is on a mission is an understatement in Daniel's case. To watch him guide folks to some of the most beautiful locations on Earth while leading them towards profound experiences and perspectives few will ever witness is breathtaking. There is so much more to gain through this man's writings and teachings. Whether it's from watching him speak on stage, reading a book, experiencing a guided meditation via a video gathering, or if you're fortunate enough to accompany him on one of his sacred journeys, I promise it will be well worth your time."

—**ADAM KING,** Tesserean.com

"This book is a must read!!! I had the honor and privilege of traveling to Peru with Daniel on a mindfulness journey, and the experience was life-changing! I am mindful and present in all I do thanks to Daniel."
-Francisco Cortes, President & Co-Founder of The Setroc Group, Inc.
"Daniel shares a deeply personal journey, filled with transformational wisdom and practical tools, on how to live a radically mindful life. I've personally witnessed Daniel move from being a successful but stressed out and miserable businessman to a mix of coach, shaman, speaker and yes, still a businessman who now lives with a daily smile on his face and peace in his heart. It's been a magical journey to witness, and I am so happy that he is now sharing it with the world."

—**Eva Charlotte,** Speaker, Writer, Humanitarian, Founder and CEO at R.I.S.E & Global Peacemakers

"Daniel opens his heart and takes us on an inspiring journey of discovering truth and wisdom within, helping us connect as one with every moment."

—**Saul Alvarado,** Corporate Vice President

"As my mindfulness coach, Daniel's coaching was instrumental as I navigated the selling of my company. His thoughtful insight was pivotal during my transitioned into the next phase of my personal and professional life. His impact was especially poignant in recognizing and creating opportunities for myself as well as turning barriers into roads paved. The practices and steps to *Radical Mindfulness* were instrumental in my overall success and encourage you indulge in his wisdom."

—**Josefina Bonilla** President and Chief Diversity Officer Color Magazine

RADICAL
Mindfulness

Profound Inner Peace—
In As Little As 60 Seconds

RADICAL
Mindfulness

DANIEL GUTIERREZ

Foreword by PARTHA NANDI, MD FACP

Radical Mindfulness

Condor Press

ISBN: 978-1-7336608-0-8

Library of Congress Control Number: 2019901070

In Memory of
Catalina Gonzales Ruiz

TAKE FLIGHT

Take flight, dear mother.
It is sad that you are no longer with us.
Our hearts break at the thought
of not having you to lean on, laugh, or cry with.
We know you are not completely gone.
However, this human condition doesn't let go easily.
Fly, my dear mother, and let your spirit soar
like the Andean condor way above my beloved
Machu Picchu.
You are free now, from pain, sorrow, and sadness.
Bask in the powerful love of the Divine
and those who have transitioned before you.
Greet and embrace them and let them know
I will see them someday,
but not now
as I still have work to do here.
Fly, mother, fly.

—Daniel

In Dedication to

My son,

Aaron Daniel Gutierrez

Your life has added color to mine,
given me the courage to get up every day,
and leave a legacy not only for you
but for the entire world.

Your big heart inspires me to open and
share more of mine each day.

CONTENTS

Acknowledgments

So many people have been a part of making this book, way too many to mention. However, there have been some key angels who played a huge part in my journey to *Radical Mindfulness* and the completion of this book.

To Monica and Dean Davis, Aaron's mother and step-father, who have given me the space I needed to complete this project while making sure our son always had what he needed. Their actions did not go unnoticed.

I want to thank Jan Edwards for support in making this book a reality. She didn't pressure me and allowed the story to come out as it was supposed to, yet, with her editing magic, brought my words to life!

I want to acknowledge the Evolutionary Business Council, especially Teresa de Grosbois, who always reminded me of my own greatness and the part I play in the big world of ours, and Kathryn Guylay, who stood by my side and guided me during this process.

I want to also acknowledge the Long Beach Holistic Chamber of Commerce members and the Holistic Chamber of Commerce International. It is because of their love and cheering me on that I was able to stay focused.

A special thank you to the founder of the HCC, Camille Leon, and members Scott Ware and Chantalynn Huynh who gave me their undying support.

I also want to thank those special people in the sacred valley in Peru who made this spiritual journey I am on so magical. Their love and support and their teaching me the way of the Quero and Inca culture allowed me to spread my wings and learn my place in this world.

I thank my dear friend Lydia Colón Perera and her husband, Roberto Perera, who opened their home, Quilla Villa, and network and showed me love—and tough love when I needed it.

I thank Lesley Myburgh, who created the space to work with plant medicine with love, grace, and support.

I thank Mimi Pacheco, who is always there to support me in whatever I need. It's hard to find friends who really appreciate you.

I thank my nurse, Cecilia Muniz Maldonado, who not only takes continual care of me and my travelers but is also a great friend.

I thank Carlos Felipe Escobar Alvarez and Alicia Salinas Quispe, who have opened their hearts and shown me the way of the people of the Sacred Valley of Peru. Each and every one of these people has been instrumental in my bringing this book to completion.

Last but not least, I want to acknowledge my dear friend Melissa Botten, who truly stood by me through my mother's death as a pillar to lean on when I needed it. I know Mom sent this special earth angel to be my guide.

An Explanation of Important Terms

The back cover of my book describes me as someone who went "from boardroom executive to medicine man." In your mind, you might picture someone in native ceremonial dress with a large feather headband, long black hair, and an assortment of medicinal potions and native tools by his hands.

The kind of medicine I am talking about is the kind of medicine that is good for the heart and soul: the medicine of love, compassion, understanding, acceptance, and forgiveness, and the ability to know when and how to use it. I am also referring to the medicine of spirit, connection, and the gift of knowing things. In this book, particularly in chapter two, you will discover more about why I have been called a medicine man.

Throughout this book, I use the words *God*, *Divine*, *Source*, *Creator*, *Universe*, *Spirit*, *Nature*, *Essence*, and *Pachamama*. Please do not feel offended or dismayed if they do not resonate with your beliefs. I use them as different words for the same thing: spirituality and connection to God and all that is. Feel free to insert whatever word, name, or term you feel comfortable using that makes you feel good. These words I use are not in any way intended to create any judgment or persuasion of religion or faith.

FOREWORD

*Are you curious to know how you can find peace
and tranquility in as little as 60 seconds?*

I was five years old, and it was early Saturday morning. My mother and father prepared the room for our daily prayers. My sister and I, along with my parents, loved this time and cherished our prayer room. It was tranquil, bringing stillness to the mind, body, and soul. I have asked for help and clarity in that room so often in my young life, guided by meditation and prayer. Spirituality was a way of life as long as I can remember. As a young boy in Kolkata and Bangalore, India, I was taught how important spirituality was in our lives. As a young medical student in Detroit, Michigan, these experiences helped me understand the importance of the healing craft of medicine. As a physician in the United States, the power of these techniques was incredible in helping my patients in their fight against crippling diseases; so powerful was this effect that I outlined many of them in my international television show along with my books, writings, and keynotes. Physical and spiritual health are equally important, and using the tools of spirituality can help so many individuals achieve health and wellness. I have witnessed this first hand in my patients, whether they were fighting autoimmune disease, heart disease, depression or addiction.

Mindfulness has been practiced for centuries and is an essential tool for many cultures. In *Radical Mindfulness*, Daniel Gutierrez gives the blueprint to true spirituality. He beautifully outlines how to adapt our lives to be radically mindful! Not only does he shows us how to align our thoughts, intentions, and actions, but do it on an almost continual basis; now that's radical! Awareness by itself is critical, but with Radical Mindfulness, Daniel couples this awareness with action and defines it with commitment and consistency. His journey to true self-realization is quite compelling. As a son, husband, father, and brother, I empathize with his soulful experiences and love his methods of integration into Radical Mindfulness.

Rarely has such a successful entrepreneur made the trip of a lifetime, showing us how material success does not always match spiritual wealth. From his personal experiences as a world-class speaker and thought leader, Daniel shows us all that our society's symbols of success may not lead to true wealth of the soul. By helping us to rid ourselves of our ego, Radical Mindfulness leads to a practice where awareness leads to actionable results. For anyone yearning for a deep and lasting love affair with your soul and mind, this work is a must read!

I met Daniel Gutierrez in beautiful Costa Rica as part of deep dive workshop organized by the Evolutionary Business Council, started in 2010 by Teresa de Grosbois to assist in bringing influential like-minded individuals together to expand global change. It was there that Daniel told me about Radical Mindfulness. Radical Mindfulness is a lifelong practice that is true whether you are a corporate executive or an individual looking for more peace and tranquility in your life. Learning to stop and breath, before you act, has a profound result in all areas of your life. If you find yourself paralyzed from fear, doubt, and disbelief, these techniques can be life altering!

In our society, we face a crisis of social isolation. Suicides are at an epidemic level. Death from opiate abuse is at all-time highs. Treatment advances are being made but are not adequate to handle the tragedies that occur every single day in our nation and the world. Radical Mindfulness is a great tool to help so many of our sisters and brothers, our mothers and fathers. By adopting spirituality to the miracles of modern medicine, we can help so many live healthier lives, physically, mentally, and spiritually.

I hope you are inspired to achieve a greater sense of peace and tranquility. Taking as little as 60 seconds will lead you to 120, 180 and maybe 240 seconds; leading you to a powerful practice of Radical Mindfulness for a life-time. Namaste.

Partha Nandi, MD FACP

CEO & Creator

The Dr. Nandi Show, Emmy award-winning television show

International Best-Selling Author, Ask Dr. Nandi: 5 Steps to Becoming Your Own #HealthHero for Longevity, Well-Being, and a Joyful Life

Detroit, Michigan 2019

CHAPTER 1

The Awakening

*"And what do you benefit if you gain the
whole world but lose your own soul?"*

— Mark 8:36

I was at the pinnacle of what most would call success—
*at least what I, from a small, rural Texas town, called
success.* Close your eyes for a minute and visualize this
with me.

The year is 2011. The place, New York City—the Big
Apple. I'm a successful international corporate consultant
and motivational speaker, pulling in up to $25,000 per
keynote speech, teaching Fortune 500 company executives how to harness their thoughts, improve productivity, and be inspired to stay focused and achieve their
dreams. I'm a radio show personality and author of a few

books, including *Stepping into Greatness: Success is Up to You*. I've been featured on magazine covers and named one of *Latin Business Magazine*'s "Top 100 Hispanics in America." Honored to host the Sol Awards, I was recently interviewed as one of eighteen world-renowned scientists and transformational thought leaders for the documentary film *Luminous World Views*. I've been inducted as the president of the prestigious national leadership organization PRIMER. I assisted Mexican President-Elect Felipe Calderon in facilitating outreach to the U.S. media and business community. And I was an advisor to the Department of White House Personnel for the Obama administration. Known for transforming businesses and individuals all over the world, I teach that anyone can be, do, or have anything by understanding the 7 Golden Rules to Success.

I'm in Manhattan for a monthly gathering and business meetings and just finished dinner at a swanky, private, membership-only club in Manhattan on the thirty-ninth floor of 666 5th Avenue. The Grand Havana Room is the kind of place that really oozes success, designed for the privacy of its patron athletes, politicians, and celebrities to wine and dine with the world's best. Sitting in a posh leather chair next to me were a prominent politician and a well-known athlete. I'm in my custom-made, $1,700 suit and well-shined shoes, smoking my Cuban cigar, and sipping a $250 cognac, the best money could buy.

Watching the large puffy snowflakes fall thirty-nine floors to the streets below, I think, *This is it. Success at its peak. All my life, I dreamed of being right here in this very spot. What else could I ask for?* As my thoughts drift with the snowflakes, I see my reflection in the window, and a voice speaks to me.

And what values did you sell to get where you're at? Is this really who you are? Are you happy, Daniel? Is this the success you wanted? Are you playing a game?

As I stare into the abyss of the snowy night, my eyesight fogs. Tears begin trickling down my cheeks.

THEY CALLED IT GOD

As far back as I can remember, maybe six or seven, I knew that I knew things. I could feel energy, read people's hearts. I knew their emotional state and what they were experiencing. I didn't know what all of it was or what to do with it though. I never heard anyone else talk about those kinds of things, so I didn't either. But that knowing was always a part of me.

I was brought up Christian, but we didn't go to church because it was the right thing to do. We went to church because we got hot meals and were surrounded by people who showed us love. Church was a haven for me, a place where I found a lot of love, acceptance, and belief. It wasn't that Mom didn't show love. She was a very loving being, and I was her *Danny Boy,* but my relationship with my stepfather kept me out of the house more often than in. We fought daily. If what I felt at church was God, I wanted more.

On a couple of occasions, I was invited to give the talk in church. When the time came for me to call those who wanted to give themselves to Jesus, lots of people came up. The church convinced me I had a gift. They saw something in me. They saw goodness in me. They called it God. They called it Minister. *But who was I?* I was just Danny Boy.

They gave me a license, and, at seventeen, I became a licensed Baptist Minister. I had a sense of purpose. To be closer to God.

I studied the Bible in Hebrew and Greek at Bible University in Texas and became president of the men's Bible study. One fall Sunday, I was scheduled to speak at one of the churches, broadcast live on the radio. The night before, I was invited by the other ministers to attend a party. Without going into detail, what I witnessed that night literally floored me.

After a sleepless night, I stood in front of the entire church ready to speak, and my heart suddenly broke. I couldn't do it. I was devastated by what I had seen the night before. If that was what the church and ministry were about, I wanted no part of it. On a live radio broadcast, I said my piece and I quit. I walked off the stage, out the church doors, and never looked back.

Before that day, I had known God in a way I would never again know God. My faith was gone—in God and in man. If the truth be known, nothing—*and I mean nothing*—could fill the hole left from disconnecting from myself, my church, and my creator. The hole left an emptiness I would spend many years trying to fill with human stimulants and other substitutes. Danny Boy was no more.

THE SACRIFICE

The day I left that pulpit, I quit Bible University and I went straight to a liquor store. That day marked the beginning of a drinking party that lasted for five years as I tried to push all the hurt down. But the wound was so deep and wide that no amount of liquor could numb the pain or fill the holes. I was floundering with no purpose, no church, no community, no love. I felt lousy. It was all a lie. Nobody really cared.

If there was a God—*and I doubted that now*—I was damned angry with him for what I had experienced. How could God betray me? So I went on drug binges and mixed in all assorted substitutes for love and comfort. In fact, half of my twenties was spent trying to end my life. On two or three occasions, I tried to overdose on drugs but woke up in the emergency room still alive. I thought, *I can't even get that right. I can't even kill myself.*

Until one day when I woke up and saw my life as if I were seeing it for the first time in five years: on a course of self-destruction that would eventually take me down. *How did I get here?* With that awareness, I quit the drugs and the alcohol. Cold turkey. I straightened myself up and decided I was ready to grow up and face the world.

Best Buy had only fifty stores at the time and needed people who were willing to be mobile and help the company grow. So, I decided to leave my small Texas town of Midlothian and build a company and a future. Like Jimmy Stewart in *It's a Wonderful Life*, I was full of energy and hope. I wanted to see firsthand what the big world had to offer. I was certain that if I had a chance to experience what society called *success*, I would be happy, and I was convinced there was no way I could reach the level of success I was looking for if I stayed. Eager for the rich life I dreamed of, I kicked the dust off my shoes from my little country town and set out on a journey to discover the world and make a name for myself.

After joining the executive team and successfully building Best Buy's chain across the United States, I pursued the entrepreneurial business world. It was a fast-moving life. I always seemed to be in a hurry to get here and there. I worked very hard and slept little. I became a student of motivation and positive thinking and a practitioner of neuro-linguistic programming, then a certified seminar speaker and coach. It didn't happen as fast as I had wanted it to, but it happened. I went from being near homeless at one point to speaking for food, calling myself "Meals on Wheels." Finally, I was making fifty dollars an hour and, eventually, as much as $25,000 an hour as a keynote speaker. You've read the gist of the rest, and more details are in my other books.

I think we all grow up wanting to be successful. I was sure that if I could experience success, I would be happy. I would have arrived. *Arrived where, exactly?* I had reached the top, that pinnacle of success the world had lured me to when I was young. I was here. *So, why did I feel so empty?* Where was the love? Where was the compassion? The understanding? The forgiveness? The only thing I had was the desire to succeed. *But that world was all an illusion.* Where was I? Who was I? Where was Danny Boy, the dream-filled boy from that small town in Texas? Were my friends real? Or were they around for what I could do for them? Or was I around for what they could do for me? *What price had I paid for this hollow life?*

As I sat in that posh chair on the thirty-ninth floor of The Grand Havana Room, suddenly nothing was clear anymore—except one thing: I needed to stop. *I needed to find out who I really was.* My true self. My passion. *What did I really want?* I needed to reevaluate.

I was in my late forties. *Could I recover?* My term as

president of PRIMER was coming to an end. It might actually be the perfect time to remove myself and step away from all national and international leadership and board positions. What about my speaking career? *I was known as an expert on success, but I didn't know what that meant anymore.* I needed to redefine that for myself.

On that cold night, sitting in my $1,700 suit high above the snowy streets, I decided to let it go. *Let it all go.* I decided to set out on another journey, a different journey—into the unknown. Not to speak or teach. Not to motivate or inspire. *My new mission was to be inspired.* To learn. This new journey would lead me on a three-year quest in search of a deeper meaning. A deeper connection. A connection to truth. A connection to me. A quest to discover who I was. A quest to find my place.

A quest to find my purpose.

CHAPTER 2

A New Journey

The instructions for your life are within you.

This quest opened a brand-new world to me—a world full of diversity and cultures that beckoned me. I discovered other ways of life, other religions. It's not that I was seeking to know religion; *I was seeking to know truth.* It mattered not where or how that truth came but that those who believed in that truth knew it from an authentic, genuine, and deep inner place.

I read about different methods, beliefs, and ceremonies to connect to the Divine. I studied many teachings, from Jesus, Buddha, Islam, and Taoism, to Confucianism, Te Ching, and Hinduism. I studied spiritually ascended masters like St. Germain, Krishna, Metatron, and Kuan

Yin. I reveled in documentaries on Tibet, global warming, and the ways of the mind, like *What the Bleep Do We Know!?* and *The Secret*. All of these sources of study promised the gift of Truth I was looking for.

Each journey, each book, and each film taught me things that seemed to be already circulating somewhere inside me. I knew the truth I was seeking was already in me, not with someone or someplace outside of me. But I needed to know how to access the truth in me. I needed to be willing to trust in it. I developed deep meditation and mindfulness practices that taught me to calm my mind and listen to the still-knowing voice inside that knew the answers. I didn't know why, but—*just as I knew that I knew things as a young boy*—I knew I had to do this. I followed the Divine breadcrumbs that began to guide my path.

NEPAL

One of the first places I landed on my journey was the Himalayan state of Nepal. I had always been drawn to mountains, but it wasn't until I saw the majestic Himalayas that I began to understand why. At first sight, something deep inside me seemed to awaken that I could l not explain or understand. It was as though I knew these mountains and these mountains knew me. Their energy made me feel alive. And, even more inexplicably, they seemed to have the power to awaken memories within me of times from the past. Times before this lifetime. The strange thing was, I didn't even believe in past lives. But where else could these memories and feelings have come from?

I later came to learn that, as humans, we can recall only what we have previously experienced. If I recalled a memory, whether I knew where it came from or not, it was only possible for me to recall it because I was drawing from a personal experience.

What we experience in our past lives we bring into our current lives.

I immersed myself in all of Nepal's richly diverse cultural ceremonies and ways of life. The experience changed my life. Two very distinctive memories from that journey have stayed with me. On my drive up the hillside to visit the Kopan Monastery, high in the hills outside of Kathmandu, something felt very familiar, even though I had never been there. I would call the sensation *eerie*. When the monk was showing us around and explaining their daily routines and mission, I could not keep my mind from wandering into the mystery of that familiarity, contemplating explanations for the feelings I was experiencing.

At one point, I stood next to a monk in front of one of the *stupas* (Sanskrit for "heap"), hemispherical structures used as places of meditation that contain relics (śarīra:

"typically the remains of Buddhist monks or nuns").* I said, "I feel like I have been here."

His response nearly knocked me over. "Brother, you have. Welcome home."

Yet, I understood what he meant. *I had been there before.* Maybe even as a monk. I felt a deep attraction to Buddhism. Perhaps that was why. Whether I knew where it came from or not, it was only possible for me to recall it because I was drawing from a personal experience. I had no reason to doubt it or question it. Only to accept it as my truth. It felt good. It felt real. It felt right. And it resonated deeply with me.

On my last day in Nepal, I was given the privilege of taking a flight in a chartered plane to see Mount Everest and have an up-close look at the Himalayas. I had always been fascinated by Mount Everest and had read and seen many books and movies on explorations to the top of the world. Though I never had an inclination to climb it, I was excited to see it up close.

What occurred that morning as we waited for our plane would teach me one of my biggest life lessons. It would help me understand, on a deep level, my compelling and sudden departure from my successful career and leadership status.

---

* "Stupa," Wikipedia, last modified Nov. 3, 2018, https://en.wikipedia.org/wiki/Stupa.

We arrived very early in the morning, just as the sun was rising. The air was chilly, but the excitement of seeing one of nature's most glorious wonders made it unnoticeable. While we were standing outside the airport, I saw a large plume of smoke and fire off in the distance. I asked my guide if he knew what it was. He didn't, but he went inside to ask. When he came out, his face revealed he did not want to tell me something.

The flight that had left before ours had crashed. All the passengers were dead.

On the outside I tried to keep calm, but on the inside I was terrified. Had this been at an airport in the US, we would have immediately been surrounded by hysteria, emergency medical vehicles, and media. The airport would have been shut down, and all arrivals and departures would have been canceled. People would have been frantic. But here it was as if nothing had happened. There was no commotion. There was no noise.

My western mind-set had barely digested this when the loudspeaker announced it was time to board our flight. I didn't want to get in, but my mind immediately began trying to soothe me by rationalizing the odds of that kind of tragedy happening twice in one day. I swallowed my fear and boarded the small chartered plane.

As I passed by the pilot, I asked, "What caused the plane to crash?

"Pilot error."

"What company manufactured the plane we're on?"

"Boeing."

I felt better. As I took my seat, a hundred things were going through my mind. If it weren't for the plume of smoke, we would not have guessed a plane had crashed and no one had survived. All was quiet, peaceful, and beautiful in Nepal.

The Nepalese believe in the state of impermanence, that everything is temporary, that everything comes to an end. They feel no need for reaction, mania, or media, or belief in doom and gloom. They see all events and circumstances as a natural part of life's course. There is a kind of peace and beauty in that spiritual knowing that relieves them of suffering.

The day had blessed us with unusual clarity and crispness and a view of the entire mountain range. According to the pilots, that was rare. Words cannot describe the beauty. I felt an incredible and intimate connection seeing the sacred and majestic Himalayas up close. For me, it was an extremely personal experience, a familiar resonance I was just beginning to understand and accept as real.

The lessons of that journey in Nepal have stayed with me to this day, etched into my heart and mind. I had a new understanding of life: everything comes to an end, whether by death or separation. So, why suffer? I need not feel bad or guilty for deciding to leave my familiar world for an unknown world. This was my path, my journey. I needed only to be present in the moment of each experience, to learn the lessons.

These lessons would come to serve me later, and forever, in ways I could never have anticipated.

MYSTICAL PERU AND THE ANDES

I had traveled to Peru with a friend many years earlier and had loved it so much I decided to return. It was one of the most profound and powerful journeys I have ever had the honor of taking. Peru is a magical land, not only because it contains one of the seven wonders of the world, Machu Picchu, but also because it is the land of the indigenous Quero and the ancient Incas.

My deepest learning and understanding of my life path have come from my journeys to Peru. Something in me awakened, similar to what I experienced in the Himalayas, but different. It was more like an awakening of the gifts I had known as a child, those gifts deep within me I had stuffed away. Throughout my life, I had been able to read people's emotional states and understand what they were feeling. It mattered not what the mouth was saying as the lips moved because I was reading the true intentions their heart energy was radiating. I never dared to tell anyone or talk about it for fear of being ridiculed. I had never heard anyone else talk about such things. And I didn't understand why it was happening to me or how it happened, so I just kept it to myself. Until one deeply profound experience in the Andes when I began to truly understand my path and role in life.

WACHUMA

From the day I walked away from my previous life, my desire for finding truth grew more compelling and vital to my survival. My awakening to my inner connection with ancient wisdom began in the Himalayas, but one particular journey in Peru would change my life forever.

I had been staying at the home of my friend Lydia Colon Perera. Quilla Villa was a mystical retreat center perched high up on the front of the Pachatusan mountains in the sacred valley of the Andes with breathtaking views of the valley below and The Sanctuary of the Lord of Huanca. The sanctuary became a sacred place for me, where I would visit many times each year to pray. I prayed for our world and for the people around the globe who had bestowed prayer requests upon me and aspirations for me to deliver.

On my many trips to Peru, I had heard of a powerful plant medicine called San Pedro ("Wachuma" in Quecha). San Pedro is considered a master plant, or "Grandfather," because of its ability to connect man to nature and open him to himself, to seeing and understanding who he is and his mission in life, to open his heart, to heal him, and to reveal deeply hidden questions about life. This medicine was administered during the day so one could feel, see, and experience in daylight the sacred ceremonial connection to Mother Earth ("Pachamama"). I knew nothing about plant medicine and had always closed my westernized mind to anything that could be considered a drug or mind altering. I had been told not to worry and that—one way or another—the medicine would call me and I would know when it was time to participate in the sacred ceremony.

As life would have it, on one cool, calm day, Wachuma did call me. On that day, I felt its deep pull calling me to dance and experience it. I decided to listen. We assembled on the front lawn of Quilla Villa and were joined by one of the most revered shamans in Peru to perform the ceremony. Since that first time, I have come to know many healers and teachers who perform wachuma ceremonies ("Wachumeros"), but I know of none more graceful and beautiful than my dear friend Lesley Myburgh, whose life's work is performing these ceremonies with "Grandfather" around the world.

Lesley began by asking all of us to either set an intention or ask a question "Grandfather" would answer sometime during their ceremonial journey. My palms were sweating, waiting and wondering when I would be called. At long last, it was my turn. I was finally going to be able to ask the question I had wanted to ask my whole life:

How am I able to read hearts? How am I able to access unspoken information about people and their lives? How am I able to recall situations, times, and places I have never been in?

After we declared our individual intentions and questions, she handed each of us a glass of slimy liquid, the medicine she had lovingly brewed. She asked us to drink it and told us it would take about forty-five minutes to take effect. She warned that some of us would purge and some would not, but not to fear, because whatever came out was what we needed to release, a natural part of the healing. After we took our doses, we were guided to sit, relax, and enjoy the journey.

I sat in front of Quilla Villa facing the Pachatusan mountains. My mind and ego began a duel, like two massive bulls fighting in a china shop, challenging me to doubt my decision. Soon, the battle gave way to the most beautiful sensation of love I have ever experienced in my life. I could feel my heart opening and everything around me seemed to come alive. I could feel the connection to Pachamama, Mother Earth. It was like the scene from *The Celestine Prophecy* where they saw the radiating energy of the plants.

THE CONDOR

Over and over, I kept hearing myself asking my question. Then suddenly, a huge, powerful Andean condor appeared in front of my eyes. I looked around to see if anyone could see what I was seeing, but everyone was on their own journey, oblivious to everyone around them.

"I have answers to your questions," the Condor said. *"You have been a healer, teacher, and medicine man for many lifetimes. Look up at the mountains, and I will show you."*

As I gazed up at the majestic mountains, I saw a line of people walking along the top of the mountains carrying torches. The line had gaps between groups of people and seemed to go on forever.

"This is your bloodline. You have brought that knowledge into this lifetime. That is why you can see, and feel, and know the things that you do."

I began to cry. This knowing resonated deeper in my heart and soul than anything I had ever known before. This was my truth. The truth I had desired to know for so many years was now revealed.

"But what would I do with this?" I asked. *"I am just a simple man."*

"It is time for me to go." The condor flexed his huge wings and said, *"I will leave you with this. Trust your wisdom."*

That day marked the end of the old me, never to return. In the coming days and years, more would reveal itself, but those few hours in the Andes Mountains of Peru became the juncture to my new path. I had never felt more certain or clearer than I had after that experience, and there was no going back to the me I used to be. Many more answers were to come, but that day was the day I began learning to trust myself and the wisdom within me.

MY PATH UNCOVERED

Through the years of my journey to my new world, I began to develop my own daily practice for experiencing peace and tranquility. I incorporated many of the teachings I had learned from the Buddhist monks in the Himalayas and from working with the Amazonian and Andean Shamans, like meditating, paying attention to breathing, understanding impermanence, feeling love for every living creature, experiencing sacred ceremony, working with Palo Santo (sacred wood), trusting my wisdom, and feeling love and respect for Pachamama.

As I incorporated each new piece of knowledge, tool, method, and practice into my life, I also brought them into use with my clients. Though I had left my speaking career during these years of my journey, I had amassed a database of sixty thousand contacts and started teaching online classes on the principles of abundance and gratitude. I began teaching my clients how to use some of the principles, tools, and practices I had integrated into my daily life. As I learned more about myself, my truth, and the ancient wisdom circulating in my blood, my classes evolved into teaching mindfulness, which led to private coaching sessions on mindfulness, abundance, success, and the application of the principles for each.

When I set out on my quest for truth in these destinations around the world, I had no intention of creating a business out of it, but, in the sharing of my discoveries with them, my database responded. They wanted to experience what I had experienced, learn what I had learned, and see what I had seen. They trusted me, and they wanted me to take them and show them. And the people of Nepal, Machu Picchu, and the Amazon could see my reverence for the land and its ways. They knew my heart and my connection with their ancestry, so they trusted me to bring my groups and lead them safely through their sacred lands. So, within a very short time of beginning my personal journey, I was leading groups of clients on their own sacred journeys to the places I knew best.

While one part of me remained focused on developing my personal practice of spiritual rituals and ceremonies, another part of me wondered,

> *Do I really need a regular practice? Why is it so important for me to practice these every day?*

I soon discovered that developing and integrating a strong practice was necessary not only for continuing to discover the answers to my soul's questions but also to prepare and equip me for another life-changing experience. One I never saw coming.

Chapter Three

From the Head to the Heart

*Even on what seems to be our darkest days, way
above the clouds, the sun is still shining.*

I spent twenty-three years searching for truth, peace,
and inner happiness, yearning for the connection to the Divine I'd had as a child until the day
I left the ministry. I traveled to Nepal and visited with
the Buddhist monks at the Kopan and Namo Buddha
monasteries. I learned from a Sanskrit priest high atop
a coffee plantation overlooking the majestic Himalayas.
I worked with some of the most incredible shamans,
healers, and spiritual people in the world on my journey
to the Andes and the Amazon jungle. I'd been coached

by powerful Christian ministers and well-known spiritual teachers. I learned and practiced meditation and the art of mindfulness, and I applied all of my learning to my life.

I'm not sharing this to be boastful. I am sharing this because—*in my darkest moment*—all of this experience would serve me in a way so beautiful that it would literally change my life. During my first journey into the world, looking for the pot of gold—the success that proved I had "made it"—a singular thought, forever suspended in my mind, was of my mother. Mother had been a woman of few words. In the years since I had moved away, our only conversations were on Sunday mornings. I looked forward to those calls, my only connection to my mother, to my family, and to my childhood community. Woven into those many conversations through the years was her one consistent question:

"When are you coming home, mijo?"

I was chasing my dreams and my passion. She was never happy with my answer. In my mind, it seemed she was silently challenging me. *Are you really? Or are you wasting your life?* Over the years, when I felt lost or discouraged about life or about where I was heading, I thought about my decision to leave home and those conversations. My responses to her question became a measurement of how close, or how far, I was from truly living my dreams. They were a checkpoint, motivating me to keep moving forward, even in the midst of adversity. I didn't want to disappoint her.

One day, I finally had the confidence to speak my truth:

> *"Mom, I don't know if I'm ever coming home. I'm doing my life's work. You have to share me with the world."*

After that conversation, she never asked that question again.

Is It Too Late?

The year was 2017. I was at my home in Long Beach. My mother had been sick for about two years. Her condition, cirrhosis of the liver, was progressive and terminal—something you can never be prepared for. My mother was my first love, the woman who taught me to love others unconditionally, to never give up on myself or my dreams. She was the woman who had loved me through what seemed like a mountain of flaws and mistakes. Regardless of how I felt about myself, in her eyes I was her Danny Boy.

The phone rang. I held it, listening to words I did not want to hear:

> *"You need to come home."*

I did everything I could to keep from losing it. But I lost the battle. Standing alone in my living room, I broke down and wept like I'd been hit by a runaway eighteen-wheeler.

During the three-thousand-mile trip with my son to my hometown, Midlothian, Texas, many thoughts flooded my mind. I knew this would be the last time I would see her alive. Would I regret having told her she had to share me with the world? Would I feel remorse for being so far away for thirty years? For her final years?

Though I was her firstborn, after being away so long I was an outsider, of sorts. Ironically, like my mother. The youngest sister of fourteen siblings, she had left her family to go to California. Did I remind her of herself? I never knew. My family didn't talk about anything, and my mother was a woman of very few words. The only thing I did know was that I was prepared to deal with whatever came up. I told myself it would have to be OK. *I* would have to be OK.

After what seemed the longest, most painful journey I had ever taken, we finally arrived at the hospital. As we walked into her room and she could see who we were, her face lit up, and she yelled out with excitement. Everyone jumped. She had not been animated since being hospitalized. She had not seen Aaron very much over his fifteen-year youth. He looked just like me when I was young.

As the evening wore on, all her guests left. Family members had been taking turns staying with her each night, holding the fort down. I was glad to stay with her and told everyone to go get some rest. I wanted time alone with her. I wanted to take care of her. Aaron went with the family, and my mother and I were alone.

I was so happy to be with her, but deep down I was scared. I tried to make the best of this moment we were in together as I had done all my life, through both happy and sad times. I kept the mood as light and happy as I could, wanting her to laugh. When she asked for water, I reached over to help her drink, but something on the television caught my attention and distracted me. Suddenly, my mother was yelling, *"Danny!"* I quickly turned to look at her and realized, in my distraction, I had missed her mouth and was pouring water all over her face. We both started laughing. We even did a short Snapchat video of us being silly.

It would be the last time she and I were in a video together.

WHAT WILL I DO?

It was getting late and Mom was ready for bed. She asked me to turn off the lights, and I made a makeshift bed from the tiny couch and lay down. But I couldn't sleep with the alarm noises from the machines keeping my mother alive. Every time one of those damn alarms went off, my heart suffered indescribable pain, as though I'd been stabbed, and I'd jump up, terrified that something went wrong. The pain was bittersweet. I was happy to be there, alone with her, serving her, yet scared she would die. What would I do without my mommy? Whom would I call on Sundays mornings? How would I measure my life if my mother weren't here to help me?

In a moment of clarity, it hit me that my mother had sacrificed her firstborn for the pursuit of his dreams, and I had sacrificed my connection with my mother, my family, and my home. I felt like I was five years old again, finding out my father had been killed in a car accident. Losing my mother would mean I had no parents.

FIRST EXPERIENCE OF RADICAL MINDFULNESS

At two in the morning, I was still wide awake. I knew I wouldn't get much sleep. The hospital room was cold, and I was craving a cup of hot coffee. The night nurses were not far away, but I didn't want to leave, even for a moment. I sat up and looked at my mother, wondering what she was going through. Self-pity and sorrow began to grab hold of me. Had I been a good son? Should I have visited her more often? Should I have held back from telling her she needed to share me with the world? How would I survive without her?

Each time those self-pitying thoughts crossed my mind, I centered myself and reminded myself of all I had learned, all my training. And I knew that the only moment that mattered was the one I was in with her right now. Not to stay present with her now would squander our last moments together and forever taint the beauty of her peaceful transition.

What happened next may have taken place in a few seconds, several minutes, or an hour. I'm not sure. Regardless, it would clearly and permanently transform my understanding of what it meant to be mindful, present, and aware. It would bring together all my learning and take my daily practice to a higher level of understanding and connectedness.

It would be my first experience of *radical* mindfulness.

THE GIFT OF ONENESS

In that moment of centeredness, I received one of the most beautiful, selfless, loving gifts my mother could have possibly given to me. Suddenly, I could literally *feel* her pain in my body. I could *feel* her struggle to live *as if her struggling were in me*. I *felt* her lungs' effort to breathe *as if my lungs were struggling to breathe*. And I *felt* each of her organs— her liver, her kidneys—shutting down *in my body*. I was scared. I was crying. *What's happening to me? Why am I feeling this?* The room faded away. I was no longer aware of my body, the cold room, or anything I had been watching. All of my thoughts vanished.

Out of the blue, I saw a light in front of me suspended above her body. Then I became a light, and our two lights were suspended above our bodies. We were no longer mother and son. We were no longer two separate bodies. We were no longer bodies. We were just two souls. All of the fear I had around not being good enough and not having been home melted away. I felt her immense love for me. I felt her feeling my love for her. Then our spinning lights merged in a Divine embrace. I was at one with my soul, at one with her soul, and she was one with mine. We were just two lights speaking to one another, spinning in the air as her light spoke to me:

"Before we ever incarnated into this lifetime, you made a promise to me. Your promise was that you would be here when I needed you most. That's all that matters. Thank you. You have fulfilled your contract. You are free to go."

Then, in a moment, the experience that seemed like it had lasted for hours was over. I was back in the room looking over my mother. *What? Oh my God!*

As tears cascaded down my face, I held my mother and told her how much I loved her and thanked her for blessing me with this miracle, the most beautiful, loving essence I could have ever experienced. Our two souls had shed our bodies, shed our egos, and shed our human-ness, radiating pure love and light that encompassed the entire room. We were two spirits finalizing the contract we had entered into before we came to this world. In the Divine experience of that early morning, I became a different person. A peace and tranquility filled me I had never known. I was forever changed. What a gift.

As soon as I could wrap my head around what had happened, one word came to the top of my mind and the tip of my mouth: *radical*. The level of connected-ness we had shared in that miracle morning was radical. The only way I could have manifested that is by being radically present in the moment, not allowing myself to be distracted by thoughts and beliefs or sadness and remorse, or by losing my focus in the past or future. Had I not developed and maintained a continually deepen-ing practice of all of the mindful learning and methods I had gathered over my journey, I would have gotten stuck in guilt, fear, sorrow, sadness, and other emo-tions common to the human experience. I may never have been allowed that beautiful soul-transformational moment with my mother. I would never have received the gift of the message she left me with or known about our contract. I might have carried the guilt, doubt, and uncertainty with me for the rest of my life. I would never have heard her wish for me to know that all is good and she was blessing me to move forward.

And in those moments of understanding the impact of my radical presence, the idea for this book was born. *Radical* Mindfulness.

Do You Know Me?

Mother was nearing her transition, and the hospital was not the place she needed to be. She was transported back home and resting in her bedroom. The time had come for my son and me to return to California to get him back to school, but I had to do something very important for this final part of my journey with my mother.

I had brought all the wonderful things I use in my work, including some Palo Santo (sacred wood) I had brought back from my travels to Peru. In my healing, coaching, and meditation practice over the recent years, Palo Santo and Palo Santo oils were the only two tools I had been using regularly, in fact, daily. I required my clients to use the tools as well. I had also brought my condor feathers, for smudging, and my yellow medicine bag filled with many sacred articles, including a very powerful Vogel crystal.

Over the previous two years, I had brought these with me when I visited my mother, intending to do a ceremony for her, but I hadn't used them. My family didn't understand and made fun of me. I don't think they truly knew what I did and who I had become over the last decade. At least, I thought they didn't. Past experiences from my childhood had kept me from being who I was. I was sure Mother didn't know this new version of Daniel I had become, not because she didn't want to know, but she never asked. And I never told her. I was still a bit afraid to *come out* to my family, but now I no longer cared if they made fun of me. This was for my mother. To help her release the pain. To help her transition.

It was Valentine's Day, the day Aaron and I were to leave. I couldn't sleep, so I got up early. I was going to do the ceremony but wanted to get past the thoughts of anyone caring or judging me. I had already made peace with my mother's soul. This was to honor a proper fare-well to her body. I could hear Spirit whispering, *It will be OK. Honor the human side of your mother.*

In true form, I had put on all my crystals and my medicine bag, and I had my condor feather and a huge stick of Palo Santo. Finally, I centered myself and walked into her bedroom where the hospice nurse was tending to her. No one was there but us. *Great!* I thought. *Let's do this.*

The nurse was startled at my appearance, and then she asked quietly,

"Are you native American?"

I didn't know how to respond, so, I answered, *"Something like that."*

It hurt to see my mom. Her eyes were closed, and her fists were clenched in pain.

"Mom, I'm about to do a ceremony for you, and I'm going to be using a wood called Palo Santo, OK?"

She didn't respond. As I lit the Palo Santo, the wonderful aroma began to do its work. I spiraled the sacred smoke all around her body and smudged her body with the condor feathers. Silently, I prayed to the mountains in Peru and the mountains in the Himalayas, and I gently whispered into her ear that she was free to go and fly high and free like the Andean condor.

Suddenly, she opened her eyes, unclenched her hands, and said,

"Oh, that feels so good."

I could see she was at peace. As I finished the ceremony, the nurse asked me,

"Sir, you have done this kind of work many times, haven't you, for others?"

"Yes," I replied.

"I am so glad you are here to do this for your mom. I know it means a lot to you and her, and I can see how she responded to you."

My son came in to say good-bye to his grandmother. We took one final photo of the three of us. It was time for me to say good-bye to my mother. My heart knew this would be our last good-bye. My heart knew she and I had made peace with each other that night in the hospital, but the human me, the little Danny Boy, was scared and missing my mom already. I was leaving her on Saint Valentine's day. I tried not to cry but couldn't hold back the tears, and, walking into the living room, I lost it. I broke down and bawled like a little boy. Aaron came to me without saying a word and put his arms around me.

I calmed myself and picked up my luggage to leave when my younger brother came out of my mother's room.

"She wants you to do the ceremony again."

What? In front of my family? I was terrified. But I could not say no, so I gathered up all of my ceremonial pieces and walked back in. This time, everyone was in the room: my stepfather, my brothers, my sisters, the nurse, and a few cousins. I would do the ceremony out loud this time so everyone could hear my petition and hear my prayers to Pachamama (Mother Earth) and the Divine. Once more, I prayed to the mountains of Peru and the mountains of the Himalayas and the Andean condor. I told my mother she no longer had to hang on and she could go and let her spirit soar, like the Andean Condor. *Well, truth be told, I kind of whispered that part.*

As I finished, I felt an uneasy energy in the room from my prayers. The last me my family had known was a young Christian minister. So they could hear me, I said another, more formal Christian prayer to help them feel better. A blessing is a blessing. The energy of a heartfelt prayer is universal, no matter what religion, language, or form it is spoken in.

As I finished the ceremony and was beginning to smudge with the condor feathers, Mother smelled the Palo Santo I had just spiraled over her, and—just as she had the first time—she opened her eyes and said, *"I love that."* My heart sang. Knowing she truly loved the ceremonial gifts I had given her brought so much joy to me.

Then, the still small voice whispered in my ear, *Leave her the Vogel crystal.* I paused, dumbfounded. The Vogel crystal was very dear to me, and its edges were very sharp. I didn't want her to hurt herself with it. But I knew that still small voice of Spirit, and I obeyed. I took the crystal out of my yellow medicine bag and placed it on the window sill above her bed, as someone asked what it was for. I explained that it was a very special crystal, a tool to help her transition and bless her in the afterlife.

I kept my word. I had performed not one but two sacred ceremonies for my mother. I helped her transition. My work was done. It was time for me to go. I left in peace.

Four days later, my younger sister called. Mother had passed. Just before we hung up, she asked,

"Hey, that crystal you left Mom. Do you want it back?"

I was puzzled.

"You mean the one I left in the window sill? No, why?"

She got quiet.

"She died holding the rosary in one hand and the crystal you left in the other."

I fell to my knees, weeping. I finally saw. All the little ways she had surprised me in the last days of her life. I wept with the realization of all the little ways she was saying, *I know you, and I love you.* I had never told her who I had become, but she knew. She had seen the real me. She had accepted me. She had known who I was all along. Asking me to perform the ceremony a second time was her way of inviting me to be comfortable, as me, in front of my family. It brought me back to that seventeen-year-old minister receiving permission to be me. With this final blessing from her, we had come full circle. In those last four days, her actions said more to me than her words did over my entire life. *I know who you are. Do you? Are you living the truth of who you say you are? If you know your truth, stand in it. Never forget to stand in your truth.*

I got it, Mom. *Be proud of who I am and what I have become.*

THE CONDOR FEATHER

On my trip back to Texas for her funeral, I carried a feather. This was no ordinary feather. It had been gifted to me by an eighty-year-old condor, my spirit guide in Peru. The condor is a sacred animal of Peru. I knew my mother needed to have this feather for her journey to the afterlife to be complete.

I did not tell any of my family when I would arrive or where I would go when I got there. I wanted to see my mother alone, without any distractions, without anyone else there. I walked slowly up to her casket and looked in. She looked as beautiful as I had always remembered her. My heart leaped with joy when I saw the crystal in her hand. I gently kissed her forehead and placed the condor feather between her hands on top of her chest. I could feel her presence and hear her say to me, *Well done, Danny Boy.*

The day after the funeral, my family got together for a final meal before I left to return to California. After dinner, they all decided to go back to the grave to visit Mom, but I had no need for that. Mother was very much with me. Our souls had connected. Her presence was with me. She was encouraging me to spend time alone, taking in the experiences and lessons of her transition. She even nudged me to go to Fort Worth, Texas, to look for the hat I had been looking for. So we did, she and I. And in those first days after her transition,

I discovered that the longest distance I would need to travel to be with her was the distance from my head to my heart.

CHAPTER FOUR

What Is *Radical* Mindfulness? Why Mindfulness Is Not Enough

Radical mindfulness is walking down the same path you have walked a thousand times; however, today it is not only new, but you recognize that you are the path you have been seeking.

There is no doubt my mother's passing was a life-changing experience. What we shared in the final four hours of her life was the fruit of many years of internal work, practice, learning to be still, and being fully, over-the-top present in the moment. It was the manifestation of what most have never experienced. It was *radical* mindfulness.

What nuggets were brought to the forefront of my awareness? How was it possible for me to experience that kind of connection and peace with my mother at such a critical moment in my journey and her transition?

The dictionary definition of mindfulness:

> "*the quality or state of being conscious or aware of something.*"*

Like yoga and meditation, mindfulness has been practiced for centuries and, like yoga and meditation, has increasingly become a hot topic. Incorporated into the mainstream lifestyle and taught by practitioners and masters, mindfulness—as the quality of being conscious and aware of self and surroundings—is not a difficult state for humans to accomplish.

What *is* challenging for humans to do is to be in the state I refer to as radical mindfulness.

The dictionary definition of radical:

> "*affecting the fundamental nature of something; far-reaching or thorough; over the top.*"**

---

*   "mindfulness," Oxford Living Dictionaries, https://en.oxforddictionaries.com/definition/mindfulness.

** "radical," Oxford Living Dictionaries, https://en.oxforddictionaries.com/definition/radical.

How I define *radical mindfulness*:

> "The daily practice of not only being aware, but being so deeply and consistently present in your awareness that you are monitoring your thoughts on a moment-by-moment basis while simultaneously redirecting your actions toward your intentions and commitments, and you see continuous, fundamental change in yourself and continuous, far-reaching changes in your life. As such, you are the ultimate observer of your thoughts. You are the master of yourself."

WHY MINDFULNESS IS NOT ENOUGH

In speaking at an ashram on radical mindfulness, I acknowledged I was in an ashram with yoga and meditation masters, and I honored them for their dedication. Then I asked, "After you finish your yoga and deep meditation and leave the sacred grounds of the ashram, as you pull out onto the busy road at the end of the driveway, if an oncoming car nearly hits you, do you yell at them? Become stressed? Direct an obscene hand gesture? If so, then you have no practice. The result of radical mindfulness is an inner desire for peace and tranquility that produces a knee-jerk reaction to breathe first, and then act—*or not act*."

By the surprised looks on their faces, I knew I had struck a chord.

I am not saying we as humans can do this 100 percent of the time. If we can do it 80 to 90 percent, we will be increasingly able to master our inner world and become the masters of our lives. And our world is better for it.

Looking back at when I left the ministry in my early twenties, I can see a similar pattern in the behavior of the young men and women at the party who called themselves men and women of the cloth when they were on campus yet acted without awareness, honor, or self-respect when they were away from campus or church. If we desire to experience a continual state of inner peace and happiness, we must not put on spiritual coats to attend our churches, ashrams, temples, or other places of worship only to take them off after we exit their doors.

Radical mindfulness requires that we inspect our thoughts and actions on a moment-by-moment basis in our attempt and desire to create alignment between our intention, awareness, and action between our body, mind, and spirit.

When I weighed 220 pounds, I was more than aware of being overweight and that my excess weight was causing my multiplying and intensifying health problems, but it wasn't until I become radically mindful, made a commitment, and began to do the actions needed to lose the weight that I succeeded in becoming healthy.

Mindfulness is just awareness. Radical mindfulness is awareness backed by commitment, consistency, and action.

When I sat with my mother as she was dying, I wanted to get caught up in my human ego and emotions, cry about losing her, be sad that I no longer would have a living mother and father, and blame myself for not visiting her enough and living so far away. Yet, I remembered my practice, brought myself back to center, and became so intentionally and presently focused—*on a moment-by-moment basis*—that, in that state of radical presence, I lost complete attachment to my ego's needs.

The result of having a deeply integrated practice of radical mindfulness was that I did not need to wrestle with my mind to know what to do. Within minutes, I automatically transitioned into that state. And the result was the blessing of the miracle of soul-oneness my mother and I experienced. That miracle could not have occurred had I been simply mindful. It occurred because I had developed a practice of radical mindfulness.

Awareness + Commitment + Action = Results.

Over the next few chapters, I will share how I learned and applied radical mindfulness. I will describe my *Six*

Steps to Radical Mindfulness in as Little as Sixty Seconds to stop the monkey-mind and get immediately present. And I will explain the five daily practices I developed and maintained that guided me along the way.

I am clear that there are many methods to get to radical mindfulness; these are the methods I used to get there. I am happy to hear the many ways you have found to have inner peace, love, and happiness in your daily life.

CHAPTER FIVE

6 Steps to Radical Mindfulness *in as Little as Sixty Seconds*

*Life does not guarantee us an easy ride. However,
it does guarantee that if we endure and support
our intentions with commitment, we will
see success beyond our wildest dreams.*

W hat if your life seems to be a runaway freight train? What if crazy thoughts and circumstances seem to keep you dodging bullets? *What do you do if you need to get from frantic to calm in one hot minute?*

So your mind is racing, you have looming deadlines, or you are worried about a loved one or a relationship—or the lack of one. Bills are piling up, and there seems to be no solution in sight. Now what?

We do not escape our humanness. We are here to experience this life. The ocean is not the ocean without waves, and life is not life without change or challenge. Life happens, and, when it does, it can throw you into a huge spiral of doubt, disbelief, and fear. I have found in these times that I must rely on tools that help me get refocused on the now—*where my true power lies*—and not allow stress and fear to take my emotions hostage. It is imperative to become extremely radical in bringing our thoughts, feelings, and emotions into this present moment.

I do this in many ways. Here are six steps I use to stop the crazy thoughts and get present in any moment, no matter where I am or what is happening around me—*in as little as sixty seconds*. I've been using these six steps every day to keep me radically present in this moment. Apply any one or more of these when you feel afraid, stressed, angry, sad, or out of control. You can apply them at any time in your awareness, but they work especially powerfully if you apply them in your earliest stage of stress, fear, or monkey-mind.

STEP ONE

BECOME PRESENT

Breathe

This is an exercise you can do sitting in your cubicle, standing in line at the doctor's office, or waiting to get your lunch. Make sure to set your phone or timer to sixty seconds.

Stop. Close your eyes. Pay really close attention to your breath. You can do this by feeling your breath, by following your breath with your mind as it goes through the body, or by listening to yourself breathing.

Breathe in through your nose. Breathe out through your mouth. That's it!

For many of you, sixty seconds will feel like a long time at first, but you will begin to see quite quickly that, after you complete the sixty seconds, you feel different. Most people do not fully breathe. We either breathe shallow breaths, we quietly restrict or hold it, or we don't exhale all the way. Some of us restrict our breathing all day long. When we're stressed, in fear, or anxious, it seems almost automatic to hold our breath.

Notice right now if you are holding your breath.

I had a coach who used to drive me crazy. Every year, I

would ask her what my goal was for this year. Her response was always the same:

"Breathe."

Another way to practice radically mindful breathing is by taking a yoga class. I never thought I would be saying that, but I have found yoga to be a great place to learn to breathe into my feelings and emotions, to relax and release blocked energy trapped in my muscles, and to stretch my body—all at the same time. Triple benefit!

Smell

The most powerful sense we have is our sense of smell. I believe this to be the most powerful way to get radically mindful. There are many scents you may be attracted to. Pick one or more that really resonate deeply with you. I guide my clients to use lavender, mint, vanilla, or a combination of several aromas. The fragrance I personally use, and the one I recommend, is Palo Santo and Palo Santo oils.

Palo Santo is a mystical tree, related to frankincense, that grows in South America. In Spanish, the literal translation is "Holy Wood" or "Sacred Wood." Palo Santo is traditionally used for relieving anxiety, depression, and so much more. Many enjoy it for its energetically cleansing and healing properties that are similar to sage and cedar. It creates a pleasant, fresh smoke and an uplifting scent that raises your vibration. Use it also as preparation for meditation and to allow for a deeper connection to Source.

Ignite or Pour Palo Santo

If you are using a Palo Santo stick, use a match or lighter to ignite it. Let it burn for about thirty seconds to one minute, and then blow it out. Holding the Palo Santo stick, gently wave it around your workspace, home, car, and anywhere you would like to clear the energy or bless the space. The rich smell will bring peace, clarity, and good feelings. I also use it to heal areas in my body where I feel pain. After I blow out the stick, I gently move the stick and its smoke around the areas I am trying to heal and *visualize* them healing.

If you are at work or someplace you cannot burn a stick, I recommend Palo Santo oils. There are many brands of Palo Santo oils. I prefer the pure Ecuadorian oil, carried online by a company called Floracopeia at floracopeia. com. You can find a less expensive brand, but it will not be of the same quality. For every sale, they send a portion back to Ecuador to help reforest the trees being used to harvest this wonderful sacred oil.

Put only one or two drops of the Palo Santo oil in your palms and aggressively rub your palms together. Then cup your hands and take deep inhalations of the Palo Santo. This practice will automatically bring you to your center and radically present into the moment.

Listen to Music and Ambient Sounds

I find, sometimes, that getting into that sweet space that allows me to get connected requires a little outside stimulus. Music or sounds that are great for relaxing and de-stressing me are ocean waves, a babbling brook, or sounds of the rain.

Also, listening to guided meditations helps guide me to a mindful state.

Listen to The Little Red Recorder

Before one of my trips to the Amazon jungle, I received a call from a dear friend—*and musical genius*—Adam King, asking if I would carry an audio recorder and record the sounds of my journeys in the jungles and mountains. I was appalled. I said no.

When he asked why, I explained that, in the jungle, one has to be very present to harmful animals, plants, and insects—*not to mention being present for the optimum experience of receiving the gifts of the jungle*—the whole purpose of the journey. Carrying a recorder and worrying about operating it would keep me from being present.

He asked me to hear him out:

"Think about it: 95 percent of the people you reach through social media or your database will never travel with you—not because they don't want to—because of their fear of the dangerous jungle, or their lack of finances."

He explained that if I brought ı
he would add his magical atmospl
orchestral music background to t
enhance for listeners the sense that
with me, even though they were iı
own homes. I could see his vision and the value in it, and
that excited me. I agreed.

When he called back later to ask what color recorder
I wanted to carry, whether red, gray, or black, I laughed.
"Red. If I drop it, I can see it!"

Borne out of that phone conversation was what we
affectionately call "The Little Red Recorder," which has
accompanied me through the Amazon Jungle, Costa
Rica, Machu Picchu, Nepal, Bali, and Thailand. With my
Little Red Recorder, all who desire a magical way to use
the sounds of nature to help get present can have their
own personal, mindful, jungle-journey recording. Visit
littleredrecorder.com to hear more.

Walk

When was the last time you took a walk?

It doesn't matter whether you are in a busy city or in
the countryside. There is always a place to walk. Even in
New York City, Central Park is a great place to stop and
get radically mindful. Want to take it up a notch? On your
next walk, take off your shoes and connect to the earth.
Ground yourself to Mother Earth. Allow your feet to feel

softness of the grass, the smoothness of the sand, the earthiness of the soil, and the coolness of the concrete. Be instantly present and one with the natural earth.

Dip your tongue, your hands, your face, your feet, or your body in water. Look for a waterfall, stream, ocean, lake, hose, or any running water. Even big cities always have fountains. Not only are fountains designed to be structures of art, but they are also used to taste, touch, cool, connect, refresh, and hydrate.

Focus on an Object

It may be easier to be mindful when we use crystals, rocks, stones, statues, charms, sand trays, cards, or other objects that help bring our focus to the still and present moment. As I am writing this, I have a rock near me that helps me remember my mother. It helps me to get present in the now, when my mind wants to wander off into yesterday or tomorrow.

The key is to be aware of and in the present moment, to be radically mindful, to be there more often, to stay there for longer periods of the day or night, and to go deeper. Everyone is exposed to the experiences of fear, doubt, sadness, and disbelief in our daily lives. It's what we can do with those feelings and emotions that will allow us to experience more inner peace and happiness in our lives. All it takes is sixty seconds of your day—*every day*—and, before you know it, you will have developed a practice.

Yes, it's really that easy.

STEP TWO

ASK YOURSELF: *Where are my thoughts directed right now? In the past, future, or present?*

If you're feeling out of control, stressed, anxious, or afraid, your energy is either focused in the future or on the past. Our minds begin to wonder and entertain thoughts about what we could have done better or what we want the future to turn out like. We have no power in the past or future. In order to change our lives for the better, we must practice being radically, mindfully present in this moment. It is in this moment where we can do what is needed to make sure our present is peaceful and our future follows our desires. And, in the process, we will have created a different past than we have previously experienced.

I'll give you an example. Clients have called me on the fifth of the month, worried about whether they will be able to make their rent or mortgage on the first of the following month. I am always taken aback by this type of thinking. I remind them that the type of thinking they are currently using will only make their worries come to fruition. Their current thoughts will create their future reality because it is in the present moment where creation occurs. Thoughts are that powerful. The present moment is the only time that has the power to create. In other words, they are sabotaging themselves!

STEP THREE

ASK YOURSELF: *Am I OK right now?*

Ask yourself right now: *In this very moment, am I OK?* If you are not focusing on this moment, you are projecting onto what may or may not have happened in the past or limiting your thoughts to what may or may not happen in the future. In doing so, you are making it real in your mind. *Are you OK now?* Good. Then breathe a full, deep breath in and slowly release it all the way. Repeat this as many times as it takes for you to feel your shoulders drop and your stress, anxiety, fear, or sadness begin to subside.

STEP FOUR

ASK YOURSELF: *Are the thoughts causing me to feel afraid, stressed, or out of control right now real? Are they true? Have they ever been real? Or true?*

The *Huffington Post* reported that 85 percent of what we worry about never comes to pass!* We are always taken care of. The likelihood that something we are projecting will happen is 15 percent. In the moment you are stressed, afraid, or ashamed, ask yourself: *Are the thoughts causing me to feel afraid, stressed, or out of control right now real? Are they true? Have they ever been real? Have they ever been true?*

To the person stressed or afraid of not being able to pay the mortgage, I say:

"Let it go. Get radically, mindfully present. Do the things you need to do to provide your highest ability to pay the mortgage on time."

---

* Don Joseph Goewey, "85 Percent of What We Worry About Never Happens," The Huffington Post, December 6, 2017, https://www.huffpost.com/entry/85-of-what-we-worry-about_b_8028368.

STEP FIVE

ASK YOURSELF: *Is what I'm doing right now getting me closer or further from my desired outcome?*

I've coached many people who get distracted or over-whelmed by stress in their business and personal lives, to the point they're paralyzed. They get so caught up in what may or may not have happened in the past or limited by thoughts about what may or may not happen in the future that they waste their month away by worrying, regretting, or punishing themselves. This type of thinking takes them further from their goal or desire.

What action can you take right now that will bring you closer to your desired outcome? Call the client you have been procrastinating on calling. Send the follow-up email to that prospective employer. Schedule the appointment to see the health practitioner. Call that person to help hold you accountable. Write that letter you have been holding off on. Call for estimates on that service you have been avoiding taking action on. Take some step—*no matter how small*—toward that thing you want. And know that every single thought you are "feeling" anxious about is not actually happening in this present moment. It is an illusion you are making up. STOP!

STEP SIX

ACT! DO SOMETHING TO SHIFT THE PHYSICAL ENERGY AND STATE YOU'RE CURRENTLY IN.

This step is designed to break the unwanted stuck energy you find yourself in. Take a walk. Work out. Walk your pet. Go shopping. Get in the car and take a spontaneous ten-minute drive. Get a massage. Take a shower. Open the door and step outside. Turn on the music and dance. Jump up and down five times. Stretch. Stand up from your chair right now.

In changing what you're doing right now by doing something physical, you will shift both your physical and emotional energy, thereby allowing yourself to become present. It is then that you will realize the power you have in the moment to change your direction and your outcome!

Most people believe they need to be doing yoga or meditating at an ashram to be able to be fully present. *The truth is, all you need to do is give yourself sixty seconds to connect. Are you worth sixty seconds? You better believe you are!* The benefits of stopping for even sixty seconds and getting present can have profound results in your health, your business, and your relationships. You can practice all six of these sixty-second steps or just one of them. Whatever works for you is the right step for you. Use these steps to bring you radically back to the present.

CHAPTER SIX

Practice 1: *Connect: To Essence, To You, To Others*

Stress and fear were the product of not being radically mindful, a direct result of our inability to stay deeply present in the now.

THE PRACTICES

It is very important to both practice mindfulness and develop a mindfulness practice. Remember, the difference between mindfulness and *radical* mindfulness is the practice of mindfulness as deeply as possible, on a moment-by-moment basis, for as much of the day as possible, and consistently. In so doing, we become the ultimate observer of our thoughts.

You may be wondering why we need to practice at this level. Life is not life without change and problems. If we meditate, practice yoga, recite affirmations, and whatever other methods we use to get centered only once a day but do not carry that state of being throughout our entire day, we will not be able to automatically experience inner peace and balance when something surprises us or goes in an unexpected or undesired direction. We will go into flight, fight, or freeze mode and be at the control of the circumstance.

Many people lean on human stimulants like drugs, cigarettes, food, alcohol, or relationships to calm themselves. When used in this way, these are a temporary mask, a numbing agent for the stressful situation. On the contrary, being able to maintain a state of radical mindfulness during a stressful situation can be instant, long-lasting, effective, and beneficially transformative.

CONNECT TO ESSENCE

In my travels to the Peruvian Andes and in working with all varieties of spiritual teachers, Shamans, and Pacos, I had a particularly transformative experience at a sacred place in Ollantaytambo, Peru. Ollantaytambo is one of the oldest living Inca cities, with energy so peaceful and serene that all who pass through it are immediately compelled to deeply connect with the heart. I was with a group from Canada and the US on a spiritual journey to Puma Marca, an elevation of thirteen thousand feet and a one-hour drive to its summit. It was a beautiful day with a visibility level allowing us to see for miles and miles.

As we began our sacred ceremony and offered our gratitude to Pachamama (Mother Earth), I noticed a look on the face of Freddy, the Shaman we were working with. I wondered what he was connecting with so intently.

> I walked to him and asked, *"Freddy, what is the secret to life?"*

> He looked deeply into my eyes and, in a vibrating baritone, he answered, *"Daniel, El secreto de la vida es conectarse con Dios, conectarse y amor a uno mismo, y luego conectarse con otros. Daniel, no hay otro camino."*

> Translation: *"The secret of life is to connect to God, to connect to the love of self, and then connect to others. Daniel, there is no other way."*

I know I've been connected all of my life, even before I was a young seventeen-year-old minister. Radical connection, however, is on a whole different level. How was I able to connect with my mother at the level where I could feel her and commune with her soul in her final moments? One of the most important principles guiding my life then, now, and always, is *The Practice of Connecting with Essence.*

I define Essence as:

> *That sweet connection with a lover; or that feeling of love your dog sends you as you look deeply into its eyes; or feeling, hearing, and experiencing nature while you sit on a bench in the woods; or that moment of intense connection to Mother Earth that lets you know—without a doubt—that you have a purpose, that you're connected to the universe and all that created it.*

I'm not talking about religion. Religion is neither good nor bad; it is another topic. I'm talking about a present-moment connection with Spirit that allows us to feel the love of the Divine, the comfort when we need it, and guidance in the very core of our hearts. Connecting with Essence is part of our humanness and the pathway by which the truth of our souls and hearts expresses itself. The connection with Essence I experience today is simple and without dogma.

> I often say, *"We, as human beings, must be careful to understand that we should not be so heavenly bound that we are no earthly good."*

To really connect with the Divine, we must find those places, both internal and external, that bring us to that sweet connection. I bet you are thinking of one of your own right now. Through which of the ways I mentioned do you connect with Spirit? The goal is to discover your source of Essence and what that means to you. There is no right or wrong way. Choose only that way that brings you to a profound and radical connection.

CONNECT TO *You*

In that cold hospital room with only my mother and the machines constantly monitoring her vitals, I kept hearing Freddy's voice: *"We must connect to Essence, love, and connect to ourselves, and then connect to others."*

I must tell you that the process of *Connecting to Myself* would have been very difficult three years prior to that day, had I not made a discovery on my journey. Connecting to the Divine was just short of impossible for me. Being radically mindful was very difficult. My external human motivators and my crazy, out-of-control mind were on a loop that kept me from being connected.

We have an epidemic of huge proportions, human motivators that keep us from being and staying connected in the present moment: longings for love, friendships, self-value, success. These are not bad in themselves, as long as they are not our obsession or sole focus. That said, there are four motivators that, without maintaining a practice of radical mindfulness, can be very destructive: fear, stress, alcohol, and drugs. Three of these four are addictions that people have become conditioned to view as if they were badges of honor. All four, if ignored, have led people down paths toward destruction and devastation.

What I learned was that stress and fear were my big motivators to achieving success in my previous life in the corporate world. I decided to begin the process of being mindful of these destructive motivators, and, through my awareness and practice, released them from my life. Was success truly success if my motivators were fear and stress? The mainstream would probably say, "*Sure, why not? As long as you got there.*" That viewpoint seemed to work for me for a while—until I realized that the fear and stress were taking a toll on my health, my peace and happiness, and my relationships.

I wanted a closer relationship with the Divine, with myself, and with others. So, my motivators needed to align with my desires. I needed to be present enough to realize that stress and fear were my main drivers rather than peace and inner happiness. Stress and fear were the product of not being radically mindful, a direct result of our inability to stay present in the now. When we allow ourselves to become stressed or afraid, our energy is usually focused either in the future or in the past.

The rear-view mirror of a car is smaller than the front windshield because it is more important to see where you are heading than where you have been.

For me to really learn to connect with the Divine and myself, I had to build a personal practice of being radically mindful of my thoughts on a moment-by-moment basis. It literally took only a second for my mind and emotions to go off on a tangent that would extend into hours, days, or even months of not being present, out of alignment with my core desires, until I practiced redirecting myself to the present enough times that being present became a habit. Being radically present on a moment-by-moment basis brings your thoughts and emotions into alignment with your current goals and desires. Today, I know the power I have in the current moment to make a direct impact on my life. Stress and fear no longer have power over me.

Besides stress and fear, I had always thought alcohol was a great motivator for me. It was a big part of everything I did, from business to relationships to leisure time. It had become a huge source of what I thought was energy, confidence, and power. I saw it as part of my fuel, but I didn't see that I was under an illusion. The nature of alcohol can be very powerful and deceiving.

If this speaks to you, take a moment to get present and ask yourself, *"Can I stop drinking? Is there any part of my life that alcohol doesn't play an even small supporting role in?"* I'm not getting on a soapbox or judging anyone, and I'm not declaring the use of alcohol as right or wrong. But, for me, having a clear connection with all of that wonderful energy I had experienced as a seventeen-year-old was my core desire. In seeking to find all the human motivators that had kept me from that pure energy, I discovered that alcohol had played a huge part in my disconnection from it. So, I decided to really pay attention to my consumption for my health and for that deeper connection to my life and the universe.

Having a deeper connection requires that we take an honest look at all the things that keep us from that authentic connection with others, with ourselves, and with the Universe. If we are radically mindful of what we are thinking, desiring, and doing, and if we develop a practice of staying in the present moment, when something does happen to us—*and it will*—we will be prepared and not feel a compulsion to use dangerous motivators to feel better. Instead, we will stop, take a deep breath, get connected, and get present.

CONNECT TO OTHERS: FAMILY, FRIENDS, PARTNER, COMMUNITY, "TRIBE"

We are left with the last connection Freddy talked about, *Connection to Others*. I have to say I really didn't know what a deep connection to others meant until I had addressed the human motivators that were in my way.

There is a lot of talk about "oneness," and many movements encourage it though few know it on a deep, energetic, and experiential level. Without an authentic connection to self, there can be no oneness. We cannot give what we do not have. When we follow Freddy's recipe for true connection with God and ourselves, through radical mindfulness, we are clearly on our way to the deep connection of oneness that is beyond words.

During those years when I was not traveling, I had become very successful, to the point of building my online database of students around the world to sixty-five thousand subscribers. But in building that reach, I had buried myself in my online business, isolated in the confines of my home. I had social media friends—*about forty thousand of them*—but I didn't have any close, personal, local friends where I lived in Long Beach with whom I could call and talk, have lunch or dinner, or walk on the beach.

When my mother passed away and I came home from the funeral, I felt alone. She had been my only connection with my family. Our Sunday morning calls over those thirty years had been my only connection with the community I had known and lived in for the first seventeen years of my life. Losing my mom and our Sunday morning calls was like losing my family. I felt like I'd lost everything. I joke now that the internet almost killed me. But the truth was, *I felt alone.*

That realization prompted me to seek the kind of support that internet connections could not give me. I needed a tribe of my own. I needed human connection, eyeball to eyeball, shoulder to shoulder. I used the internet to search for spiritual groups and centers I could go to and belong to, to build the community I wanted. I'd never been a great follower, but I knew if I could find a place or a group, I could build a community to support me and each other. It would be a win-win. I would use my leadership skills to serve the local community and build my tribe.

The right opportunity presented itself to me in The Holistic Chamber of Commerce. I called Camille Leon, the founder, and asked if I could take the role of president and lead a chapter in Long Beach, California. Six months after my chapter's grand opening, I also became an official member of the board of the International Holistic Chamber of Commerce. Shortly after that, I reconnected with the Evolutionary Business Council, founded by a dear friend, Teresa de Grosbois, and became one of the advisory board members of their Wisdom Council.

From a deep yearning to connect with people on a heart level, my community grew. A few months later, I created Radically Mindful Sundays, weekly video calls that connect with people all over the world. There is a magic in being able to see and connect *live* with people from all corners of the world, sharing morning coffee with people we would never get to know in person. The community of people who plug into these *live* calls feels like an amazing connection. It's like a virtual church.

Several weeks after having these calls, a friend helped

me realize that, on a subconscious level, I had recreated the Sunday morning calls I used to have with my mother! And, before that, my Sunday mornings in church! Now, every Sunday morning—*no matter where I am in the world*—I look forward to my 8 a.m. Radically Mindful Sunday calls with my coffee and my community.

Though we may not realize it, we all need the support of a community. We may be isolated, *sometimes by choice*, by human motivators, or because we don't know how to connect. I could never have realized I had a need for community or been able to connect authentically with them face-to-face and heart-to-heart without first connecting to Essence and then connecting to myself.

CHAPTER SEVEN

Practice 2: Forgive

*Forgiveness in an external action
for internal results.*

One of the most amazing experiences I had on my many trips to Peru, in my sacred journeys into the Amazon jungle, was observing the constant cycle of unconditional forgiveness and renewal. One hot and humid day, we were invited by Marlon, the shaman we were working with, to accompany him for a walk in the jungle. He was excited to show us the many plants and the natural medicine he made from them. With each step we took, he stopped to point to a plant to explain the condition it cured. He explained that each plant was a natural medicine for just about any ailment and disease in existence, like diabetes, and even AIDS. With each step, we could feel his appreciation for the jungle's ability to renew itself and its inhabitants.

I learned that, for the jungle to survive, it has to be willing to let go of what no longer serves it through the process of forgiveness. As we walked and listened to the crunching of the old, molding branches, leaves, and fruit from the trees, we could see life making its way through the decayed matter. As we got deeper and deeper into the jungle, and with each story he told, Marlon seemed to become quieter. He had a sad story, the story of his tribal initiation into becoming a shaman—an amazing story of unconditional forgiveness.

When Marlon was just seven years old, his grandparents had brought him deep into the jungle. Always excited to spend time with his grandparents, he asked them where they were going, but they did not answer. After walking for a few hours, they stopped and asked young Marlon to wait and told him they would be back. He did not understand, but he complied.

Marlon waited and waited. It grew dark, yet they had not returned. Marlon was sad. He could not understand why they would leave him. Years passed. Still, they did not return. He knew they had left him because they did not love him.

Marlon learned the ways of the jungle and how to cohabitate with its plants and creatures. He was sitting in the makeshift hut he had made from branches and straw from surrounding trees when two huge jaguars came into his camp. He thought it would be the end of his life, assured they were there to eat him. Miraculously, they did not. Marlon made peace with the jaguars, and they slept with him every night for the next few years and protected him from the dangerous jungle.

Ten years passed. Marlon's grandparents came back. They were startled on their arrival to see the big jaguars in the camp, and they prepared to kill them. Marlon shouted out to them, ordering them not to kill them because they were his friends and had protected him.

Marlon could not help but ask why he had been left alone. Did they not love him? What Marlon had not known was that he had shown unique promise in his tribe and had been left that day to determine whether he would perish or learn the ways of the jungle: to learn the medicinal value of the plants around him, to learn to sustain himself, and to learn to become one with the jungle. The result would decipher for his tribe whether he was a true and gifted healer. His grandparents explained that the way of their people was to leave the promised one alone to learn the jungle, to see if he were truly their teacher. His survival was evidence of his oneness with the jungle and proof that he was a natural maestro (teacher) and healer, a true shaman.

After hearing their explanation, Marlon decided to forgive them unconditionally and embrace them—but not for their benefit. He forgave them for himself. He had learned that the jungle's cycle of unconditional forgiveness and renewal had kept him alive for those ten years alone, and he knew that, without forgiving his grandparents, he would be forever chained to the past and a life of suffering through holding onto anger and blame.

Like Marlon's forgiving from a place of understanding and appreciation, the act of forgiveness is an action that extends outward but has an inward result. Releasing emotions and beliefs that no longer serve us creates a vacuum for the universe to fill with new, more powerful emotions and wisdom. On that hot and humid day with Marlon in the jungle on top of Pumamarca in Peru, I learned I could forgive unconditionally and live a freer, more purposeful life.

- Love and forgive God.
- Love and forgive ourselves.
- Love and forgive others.

To be radically mindful, we must learn to forgive, beginning with God, then ourselves, and then others. In my mother's cold hospital room, I had to forgive myself and let go of whatever guilt, regret, and blame I was holding onto. It would not have been possible for me to be at one with her without letting go of whatever thoughts, beliefs, and emotions were holding me in the past or projecting me into the future. To forgive, we must get radically present.

I realize that forgiving is hard for some. I don't suggest that we condone the bad behavior of others. I only suggest that we forgive them. When we don't forgive God, ourselves, or others, it's like hoping that the object of our resentment will drink a vial of poison as we drink the poison. Forgiveness is an action extended outward that has an inward result.

CHAPTER EIGHT

Practice 3: Accept Unconditionally

*Unconditional acceptance does not
require understanding.*

If I had to condense all the learning from my journey to radical mindfulness into one truth, it would be the truth of what I had felt inside myself as a young boy: that I was different, and that I was here for a special purpose. Not having the clarity or understanding of what it all was and how or why I had it was a source of great pain in my formative years. I could never talk about it. As far as I knew, I was the only one in my family—*or my community, for that matter*—who had it. Nonetheless, the knowing was there, and it had nestled itself deep inside of me, patiently waiting.

We all have beliefs and realizations lying just under the surface of our awareness that sometimes rise up unexpectedly, causing us to feel uneasy or afraid. I find that when I'm uneasy about someone or something, it's because that person or condition does not meet my expectations, beliefs, or preconceptions. Put simply, they do not act in a way that makes me feel good. The only way I can avoid unease, to feel peacefulness and calmness, is to practice unconditional acceptance.

Of the many sacred teachings I received in my journeys to Peru, one of the most surprising was the lesson of the jungle. The Amazon can be an unforgiving place, with conditions that are very difficult to accept and challenging to endure. When I first traveled into this jungle, from Iquitos, Peru, as we ventured up the mighty Amazon, the comforts of civilized life quickly became a distant memory. I was taken aback by the stark contrast of the raw, untamed jungle from my modern-day world. We had no electricity, no refrigeration, no bathroom, no kitchen, no bed, no furniture, no television, no computer, and no cell service. Upon arriving at our destination in our makeshift boat, we were immediately greeted by swarms of mosquitoes. I had grown up in Texas and had seen my share of mosquitos, but, let me tell you, I had never seen so many mosquitos in all my life.

It was there, deep in the jungle, that my learning about unconditional acceptance really took hold and where my practice of deep breathing to center myself and avoid panic was put to the test. The jungle had established the necessary conditions for its self-preservation long before I'd ventured in. I was merely a stranger on a temporary visit. To help me stay in the present moment, avoid going into fear of the future, and be in a state of acceptance, I repeated this little mantra:

> "Universe, please help me set aside anything I think I know about my world back home and the jungle. Open my mind and heart to a new experience of this incredible world, your love, and unconditional acceptance."

As soon as I let go and stopped resisting, my heart opened, and I saw an entirely new jungle. By the end of that first Amazon experience, I realized that when I embraced the jungle as it was—*not as I saw it*—my experience changed for the better. The discomfort I had been experiencing all along was self-inflicted.

> I learned to dance in the rain *instead of wondering when it would stop.*

> I allowed myself to go to bed early *rather than wishing for a lamp at night.*

I accepted that the dangerous, venomous elements in the jungle were not there to kill me *and that they existed to protect the jungle.*

I allowed myself to relax and sleep in a hammock *and I became childlike.*

Without technology and cell service, *I opened myself to the gifts of a much-needed break, the ability to stay present, and the sounds of the roaring jungle.*

And the mosquitoes? *We learned to coexist.*

Unconditional acceptance requires that we accept things as they are, not as we would like them to be. It asks us to release the resistance against all that is and all that is outside of our control to free ourselves from our own discomfort.

CHAPTER NINE

Practice 4: Love, Be Grateful, Celebrate

What would happen if you loved the way the universal energy loves you? Your heart would expand so big that there would be no room for resistance, resentment, and revenge—just love.

LOVE!

Do you know why I love so intently and so fully? Because, when I allow my heart to lead instead of my ego, it changes me. Yes, I open myself to hurt and disappointment. But:

I would rather go to my grave having loved authentically and completely than never to have loved at all.

One of the greatest gifts my mother gave me was

teaching me to *love no matter what.* She had a way of showing us that nothing could ever change the love she had for us. Her words remind me of a Scripture:

> *"Love is patient, love is kind. It does not envy, it does not boast, it is not proud. It does not dishonor others, it is not self-seeking, it is not easily angered, it keeps no record of wrongs. Love does not delight in evil but rejoices with the truth. It always protects, always trusts, always hopes, always perseveres. Love never fails."*

> **—1 Corinthians 13:4–8**

If we follow the examples that Jesus and Buddha taught about love, we are to love no matter what. But love can be challenging and painful because we inject into its purity all our human emotions, expectations, and understanding—*or misunderstanding*—of love into our ways of loving. However, I have found that when I stay radically mindful, I am able to be more aware of when I am projecting the future or the past onto the person I am attempting to love.

I *love* everyone fully and without conditions. However, that does not mean I *like* everyone. Nor do I believe we should ever allow ourselves to be doormats or hold onto unhealthy relationships for the sake of holding onto love. One can be loved from afar as deeply as from up close.

The key to loving and being loved is to be radically

mindful, be present, and to maintain that state as often as possible. In this way, we are less likely to allow the past or the future to dictate the level of presence and authenticity in our love.

JUNGLE LOVE

From the moment I arrived in the Amazon on my second trip to visit my friend Marlon, I was struggling inside. I wanted to change my environment to meet my needs so that I could feel good. I was not happy that I had no bed to comfortably sleep in, no electricity for the conveniences of light and power, no bathroom to provide privacy and a civilized method of disposal, no shower to fully and easily clean myself, no cellular service to communicate with my community, no gas to cook my meals, and no water to refresh myself or wash my clothing and supplies.

However, by the time I left the Amazon, I had discovered what a unique and magical thing the jungle was. I had come to learn its naturally sustainable properties, respect its perfected and efficient, nature-made systems, and appreciate its powerful gifts. I had fallen in love with the jungle for what it was, not for being what I wanted it to be. That is love.

HAVE GRATITUDE!

What completely surprised me about the jungle is that it had the ability to fully sustain us. If one becomes lost in the jungle, there are trees whose branches hold enough water to cut a vine and drink from it! Because the water in the rivers and streams was undrinkable, filtered rainwater became our only source of drinking water, and it tasted really good.

The jungle had many fruits, like papaya, coconut, and bananas, and even nuts and flowers, to feed us every day. It had plant medicines that alleviated sickness and bites from animals and insects—*even mosquitos.* I learned that the jungle is beautiful and self-sustainable, without any need for interference from man. For all of this, I am eternally grateful.

Gratitude is a choice. On that snowy night in Manhattan, when I suddenly became aware of my unhappiness, I was not grateful. For anything. Life, God, and the Universe had granted me the opportunity to be in that wonderful city and in a place of worldly success, but I was not grateful. Something was missing.

I am so grateful for my life today. Every bit of it. All the good times, and all the not-so-good times. It is those not-so-good times that allow me to see life in a different way than I currently experience it, in order for me to open myself to the learning waiting for me. I am in my fifties. There was a time when I thought I would never live to see my thirties, *not only because of my destructive behavior trying to end my life*, but also because my father and two brothers had both died in their early twenties. Today, I am amazed by life and grateful each day that I get to wake up and have another opportunity to have a radically mindful experience of this wonderful world. It's not perfect, but nothing is. We only get to do this life once. I want to be all in.

CELEBRATE!

The jungle is constantly celebrating. At all hours of the day and night, you can hear the sounds of the animals in their jungle home. Monkeys, insects, toucans, and sloths squawking, hissing, and chirping. Listening intently, deep into the night, we could even hear the mighty jaguar. The sounds of the jungle were so continuous that it took a few days for us to get used to the noise, but, sooner than expected, our fear and discomfort disappeared. We danced in the rain to the sounds and fell asleep to its lullaby.

One of our final experiences was during our sacred ceremony, listening to the singing and chanting of the shamans in Spanish and Quechua. Their songs were deep in tone, filled with ancestral lessons passed down for centuries. They celebrated life and the blessings of healing and protection from Pachamama (Mother Earth) and the Divine.

earthiness and uncivilized rawness,
be one of the most amazing and
my life. We fell in love and gratitude,
reverence and appreciation, we cel-
with the mighty and powerful jungle.

Many years ago, as I sat on Machu Picchu watching the sunrise over the mountains, I wrote a mantra to help us get out of our own way and experience the beauty life presents to us:

Oh Divine, release me from the bondage of self, that I might open my heart. Allow me to express my heart freely and receive all that is good in life. Help me to see that everything—I mean everything—I could possibly desire in life is at the fingertips of my awareness. When I am living connected from my heart, it is then—and only then—that I can receive the gift of my inheritance. The peace, love, and abundance that is individualized as me, the reality of me.

CHAPTER TEN

Practice 5:
Integrate

*I used to think I needed to find myself only to
realize I just needed to remember who I AM.*

I have often heard it said that "knowledge is power." On the contrary, knowledge—*for the sake of knowledge*—without fully experiencing the knowing, is of no use to us. The power lies in the integration of the knowledge from the head to the body, behavior, and wisdom.

All my life, I struggled with speaking my truth *and standing in that truth*. When I left that small dusty town of Midlothian, Texas, and set out on my first journey all those years ago, I wanted to become successful, to make something of myself, to show the world what I could do.

89

I thought success would provide a reflection of the value I added to the world. But the success I achieved required me to act against my personal truth and values. Instead of reflecting my value, the success reflected where I had sacrificed my value and truth.

When I set out on my second journey years later, I wanted to learn my truth, to learn from the world who I was. I also wanted to know the truth of the world. I learned all those things and so much more.

I learned that mindfulness does not require spirituality. Anyone can become aware. Anyone of any faith—*or lack of faith*—of any culture, and of any belief system can practice mindfulness. It is simply the state of focusing on the present surroundings.

I learned that being one with our spirituality, *on the other hand*, requires *radical* Mindfulness. Radical mindfulness is not only incorporating the steps and practices outlined in this book but also intentionally absorbing them on a gradual, experiential, mind-body-spirit basis. I learned that a key step in the process is integrating the knowledge, steps, and practices from head to heart. Like adding ingredients one at a time into the cake batter, the result allows each ingredient to affect the outcome. If any step or ingredient is left out, the outcome is incomplete and unsatisfactory because each one is unique and essential. The result looks nothing like it started out because each ingredient is blended in, indistinguishable from its former separateness.

By integrating each of my experiences on a moment-by-moment basis, I became an entirely new version of myself, indistinguishable from my former self. Had I not integrated each piece, it would never have been possible for me to maintain the level of radical presence that allowed me the miracle experience with my mother or to continue to receive and understand the messages she left for me after she had passed.

Along my life's journey, I have had the honor to visit a homeless shelter in downtown Los Angeles. *Yes, I said honor.* What has always amazed me is that there are people on Skid Row who have PhDs. Did that high academic attainment serve them? I think not. For whatever reason, they lacked the ability to integrate that knowledge into the uplifting of their lives.

It's been said that if we integrate only 10 percent of what we learn, we will be better off than if we tried to digest everything we learn. I want to encourage you not to try to act on every suggestion in this book, though you may feel inspired to. These are my experiences, my journey, my steps. Choose the ones that speak the loudest to you. Begin by taking one or two of them into your practice and process so that you will gradually develop lifestyle changes that set you up for success. By integrating the understanding and lifestyle practice of them into your being, you will promote sustainability for yourself and your path, whatever your path may be.

After all my global truth-seeking, it was clear to me that if I had not been able to integrate all of my newfound wisdom and apply it to changing my life for the better, *and for forever*, every bit of it would have been for nothing. While my departure took me around the world, at my final destination I realized that my greatest journey was the journey to my inner self. In the process of integrating all of my knowledge and experiences into my mind, body, and soul, I came full circle, right back to me. My mother's unspoken messages were right. I never needed to find myself. I just needed to remember who I was. And be it. All of it. Always.

ANOTHER MESSAGE FROM MOM

Curious about the true cause of my mother's downhill spiral, I searched all over the internet to discover the reason for her fatty liver condition and eventual cirrhosis that lead to her passing. I discovered that the Mexican diet she was so accustomed to eating all her life was full of bad fat, sugar, and simple carbohydrates. The liver can only take so much of that kind of abuse until it becomes so congested that it's too toxic and exhausted to function.

At the time I made this discovery, I weighed 220 pounds. I was in so much pain. I had hip and lower back problems. I was getting injections to help relieve the pain. My knees were failing me and, at one point, an orthopedic doctor told me I needed a knee replacement. Essentially, I was falling apart. And my lack of health and freedom from pain were stealing my inner peace and happiness.

I was both heartbroken and elated with my discovery of my mother's cause of death. Had I known, I could have helped her reverse her health condition. But I also felt that, in the afterlife, my mother was able to guide me to the discovery. I needed to heed the call to integrate that knowledge with the wisdom of the Nepalese monks and the Peruvian Shamans, to take me into the final frontier of my life: my health. She was whispering to me, *Take a hold of your health now. Please promise me this.*

It was time to integrate and apply my radical mindfulness techniques to my health. I had never been successful at losing weight and had tried many fad diets, but now I found myself guided to the ketogenic diet, high in healthy fats, moderate in proteins, low in carbohydrates, and no sugar. What began as a diet became my way of life. Today, I am a happy 179 pounds and still losing weight. I'm working out five days a week and feel great. Most surprising to me was the realization that, without that extra forty-five pounds of pressure on my five-foot, nine-inch frame, my pain is gone!

Today, I can honestly say I feel equally balanced in

body, mind, and soul. Like the cake ingredients, if any one of these is out of line, all become out of line.

Take a look at the health of your body, your mind, and your soul, and ask yourself, *"Where am I out of alignment?"* Then take action.

Remember, mindfulness is simply being aware. *I was aware I was overweight, but I wasn't radically mindful to do anything about it.* Radical mindfulness includes our integration of the awareness and applying, on a moment-by-moment basis, what we know to get the results we desire. That is why it's called *radical* mindfulness, not basic mindfulness. It takes a consistent practice of radical presence, application, and integration.

It Isn't Rocket Science

*There is nothing more beautiful than the
expansion and expression of the heart.*

As I type the final words of this book, I'm sitting
by the window in Cappuccino Cafe, a small,
quaint, and humble cafe in Cusco Peru, looking
at the view of the cathedral in the Plaza de las Armas. I've
come a long way from that plush club in Manhattan, with
my well-shined shoes and so full of myself. It seems a lifetime time ago that I felt that still small voice speak to me
and ask, "*Who are you?*"

Had I known my life would be turned upside down,
would I have taken that journey? I can't answer that. I can

say, however, that I'm filled with gratitude for choosing to follow that voice that guided me to the Divine breadcrumbs. The view from this new vantage point is *radically different*.

The sky seems a bit brighter, the air crisper. Maybe it's not what I'm looking at that's different but rather the man who's doing the looking is different. This man has learned and integrated the true value of becoming radically present, of connecting to Essence, myself, and others, of forgiveness and unconditional acceptance, of love and celebrating life, and of gratitude and integration. This man has learned how to get radically mindful—*in as little as sixty seconds*, if necessary. Most of all, this man has come to realize that the greatest gift his mother had given him was his huge heart and the knowledge that love and compassion really do make the world a better place, including loving myself and my truth.

Many warned me that changing my life's course at the peak of my success would prove catastrophic to my career and my positioning as a national leader. They feared I would not recover and that I might appear as if I had "lost it." But I took that risk. *And I lost it.* All of it. The ego. The misplaced reverence for glitter and gold. The appearance of what I thought was success. The illusions I believed about life. The fear of speaking my truth. The idea of what a leader should look like, act like, and think like. The emptiness inside that ached for love and authentic relationships.

The longing to know if I had made my mother proud. The need to impress. The abusive eating, drinking, and cigar smoking. The forty-five pounds. The aches. The pain. *Yes, I sure lost it.*

Did it prove catastrophic? Did everyone lose their regard for me? Did my world fall apart? Quite the contrary. I have no stress in my life. I have no pain. I have no illusions. I have no regrets. I have no fears. I have peace and tranquility every day. I've traveled to some of the most sacred and beautiful locations in the world. I'm present with people, and they feel it. I have a community of heart-centered people who support me, love me, and explore life with me. I have a relationship with my mother that is deeper and more sacred than I could ever have imagined possible. Things happen easily for me now, without grit, turmoil, or sweat. I'm passionately in love and aligned with everything I do.

I'm finally doing my life's work. I lead people on sacred journeys all over the world to connect them with the opportunity for the spiritually transformational experiences I've discovered. I've created a Sunday morning community of people who share themselves with others. I was invited to host an online television show and attracted an audience of 60,000 viewers. I've been asked to speak to companies I'd spoken to before, but *for who I am now* and what I can teach them as a spiritual mindfulness teacher. I've been regarded as a *Spiritual Medicine Man*. I've written my fifth book and created an entirely new way of living for hundreds of thousands of people. I was invited to open for a meditation concert with friend Michel Pascal and members of the band Earth, Wind & Fire at one of the most famous stages in the world, Carnegie Hall—ironically just a few blocks away from that plush Manhattan restaurant where my life changed forever.

Did the risk pay off? One thousand times and counting. But don't let all of this overwhelm you or intimidate you. *This is not rocket science.* Anyone—*at any time*—can experience both the small and radical shifts they desire in their lives—*in as little as sixty seconds*, if necessary. Only one thing is required. A commitment to developing a practice of radical mindfulness.

When you strip away everything earthly that defines you, you are left with a naked soul. Then the journey to self-discovery, compassion, forgiveness, and understanding can begin. The instructions for your life are within you.

THE DEEP

There is a place called the deep,
a place of true healing.
Although you may support me and walk with me,
I must enter alone.
There, in the deep,
is the only true connection with my God,
that forgiving grace that saves me.
Although I walk alone to this place called the deep,
I know I will transmute the painful memories of
my past
into joy, and peace, and tranquility.
Then—and only then—
can we walk together,
free of the shadows of my past.

—Daniel Gutierrez

To Guide Your Radical Mindfulness Practice

As a helpful tool to guide your daily life, remove the following pages and use them as bookmarks or place them in your car, at your desk, on your mirror, on your refrigerator, in your purse or wallet, or by your bedside for the times you find yourself in fear, anxiety, regret, stress, guilt, worry, doubt, resentment, anger, or sadness.

Repeat this mantra to yourself, silently or aloud:

"Oh (insert your word), release me from the bondage of self, that I might open my heart. Allow me to express my heart freely and receive all that is good in life. Help me to see that everything—and I mean everything—I could possibly desire in life is at the fingertips of my awareness."

6 Steps to be Radically Mindful in as little as sixty seconds!

1. Get present: use meditation, yoga, breathwork, music, focus objects, and/or natural scents to help anchor you and bring you into the present moment.

2. Ask yourself: *Where are my thoughts right now? On the future, on the past, or on the present?*

3. Ask yourself: *Am I OK and safe right now?*

4. Ask yourself: *Are the thoughts I am currently having real? Have they ever been real?*

5. Ask yourself: *Is what I'm doing right now getting me closer to, or further from, my desired outcome?*

6. Act! Do something to physically shift the energy and state you're currently in.

About the Author

Once a high-powered executive and in-demand consultant who graced the covers of Latin Business, Cypen and Color Magazines, Daniel Gutierrez realized that there was more to success than a 7-figure earning potential. As President of PRIMER, a prestigious national leadership organization, and an advisor to the Department of White House Personnel for the Obama Administration, Daniel was a highly regarded and deeply revered leader. Though Daniel was listed as one of the "Top 100 Hispanics in America" along Los Angeles Mayor Antonio Villaraigosa, actor Edward James Olmos, and CNN's Soledad O'Brien, something was still missing.

To find fulfillment, Daniel decided to dedicate the next chapter of his life to becoming a Master of Mindfulness. Over the past ten years, he has led quests to the heights of the Machu Picchu, the depths of the Amazon and the top of the Himalayas. After  the boardroom, now Daniel has been guiding entrepreneurs and corporate executives in deep dive mindfulness immersions. Though mindfulness is a lifelong practice, Daniel has become known for giving life altering strategies in as little as 60 seconds. When facing extreme pressure, executives who use these techniques go from high-strung to highly productive. Daniel has even turned Wall Street cubicles from an environment of stress to spaces of productive serenity.

A beloved mentor and sought-after motivational speaker, Daniel was featured in the documentary *Luminous World Views* as one of eighteen world-renowned transformational thought-leaders.

In November 2018 Daniel appeared as a special guest for the renowned teacher, Michel Pascal, on one of the biggest stages in the world, Carnegie Hall in New York City. He addressed a sold-out crowd with musical support from Earth Wind and Fire, Madonna and Michael Jackson's best musicians. He is a bestselling author, who is excited to release his fifth book, *Radical Mindfulness*.

Also by Daniel Gutierrez:

- *Stepping Into Greatness: Success is Up to You!*
- *Building on Greatness: The Courage to Thrive*
- *Daniel Gutierrez on Mindfulness*
- *Fifty Lessons on My Path to Peace and Tranquility*

More information about Daniel Gutierrez's products and services can be found on the following pages.

To continue to be in touch with Daniel, please visit www.danielgutierrez.com and sign up for his free 60-second meditation.

About
Daniel's Coaching

Daniel is a master life and business coach. As a respected advisor, to the department of White House Personnel to the Obama administration and a best-selling author of five self-help books, Daniel Gutierrez offers practical insights and effective strategies for honing your leadership abilities, overcoming personal blocks, and achieving daily mindfulness. Daniel's approach is holistic, and he draws from his extensive business acumen and his deep spiritual convictions to guide his clients to higher levels of success than they could imagine.

**Schedule your commentary 30-minute
session with Daniel today.**
Schedule an appointment:
https://tinyurl.com/y7j8chlv

"As my mindfulness coach, Daniel's coaching was instrumental as I navigated the selling of my company. His thoughtful insight was pivotal during my transition into the next phase of my personal and professional life. His impact was especially poignant in recognizing and creating opportunities for myself as well as turning barriers into roads paved. The practices and steps to Radical Mindfulness were instrumental in my overall success, and I encourage you to indulge in his wisdom."

—JOSEFINA BONILLA,
President and Chief Diversity Officer
Color Magazine–Boston

"Daniel's coaching is phenomenal. He has a rare and strong gift for getting to the heart of what is important and has many times helped me get to the root of any blocks. Just as important, he truly cares, is nonjudgmental and easy to work with. His conference classes are magic; they often take me to meaningful places at just the right time. He has worked miracles for me. I highly recommend working with him. His books are written from the heart and reveal important life lessons."

—SYLVIA VASQUEZ,
Writer and Author – Los Angeles

"My work with Daniel as my coach and mentor on several aspects of my life has proven to have a profound positive influence in my life. He has a unique and effective way of releasing fear and returning to love. There were times of tears, laughter, and anger and moments of joy, but each time I got results that allowed me to see things in a different light and from another perspective that quickly cleared the blocks that were holding me back from moving forward in my life. Daniel's the real deal."

—PENNY PEDDIE – Canada

"Yes, how lucky I am to have found Daniel to coach me with my business. Daniel gets right to the heart of matters. His deep caring and endless optimism are contagious. Under Daniel's guiding wisdom, my business cannot help but thrive and prosper! I love you, Daniel!"

—DOROTHY MCNEIL,
Business owner – New York City

About
Daniel's Speaking

Your next event is upcoming, but do you have a speaker who can hold your audience's attention and give you the value-packed insights you want? With so many production details to manage, your speaker should give you confidence in the ability to deliver a professional, entertaining, and enlightening speech. Daniel Gutierrez leverages his experience, his infectious humor, and his deep belief that there is greatness in each of us has helped transform individuals all over the world.

When Daniel shares his real-life stories that come

from the heart, his appeal breaks the boundaries of many professions, ages, and cultures. People identify with the pitfalls and celebrations, the tragedies and the successes, the heartaches and the search for inner peace. He has over 23 years of experience speaking at corporate, private events, government functions, business, and spiritual conferences. He'll tailor his success and radical mindfulness strategies to meet your needs and ensure your audience leaves empowered.

For more information on booking Daniel at your next event: www.danielgutierrez.com

"I highly recommend Daniel Gutierrez as a keynote speaker and corporate trainer. I have participated in his engagements many times, and he literally holds the audience in his hands with his exquisite style and storytelling. He's unique in inspiring audiences to step into authentic leadership that grows your business and increases productivity among employees."

—DR. SHAWNE DUPERON, six-time Emmy Winner

"Daniel is a wonderful, dedicated speaker making a difference in many lives. There is a charisma about Dan that few people have, and you immediately feel his energy and drive to make this a better world in which to live. His heart is with and for the love of Our Lord and his expressive way of living shows in everything he does. When you get the opportunity, show up, tune in or grab him for coffee and a one on one. You will be honored and forever a changed person."

—JUNE DAVIDSON PH.D., President
American Seminar Leaders Association

Daniel inspired 3000 plus minority college students in Nashville at Opryland. He is still spoken about at

INROADS in 45 US cities. His stories, examples, and enthusiasm are often quoted on two dozen college campuses by INROADS student leaders. If you have not witnessed him first hand, bring him to your national conference or big day on campus.

—Wilson Martinez del Rio
INROADS International V.P.

About Daniel's Sacred Journeys

Our Peru journey is a unique South American experience that taps into the country's diverse and vibrant living spiritual tradition. Our travelers experience powerful emotional healing effects while reflecting on the divine Peruvian nature. We visit several amazing locations, including Machu Pichu, Lima, Cusco, and Aguas Calientes. We interact with the people of this land, who are generous and open in the sharing of their spiritual knowledge, experience, and connection. Upon  returning home, our travelers reported feeling enlightened and positively changed in how they viewed the world and, in their ability, to tap into their inner greatness. Don't miss our next amazing journey! For more information on Daniel's sacred journeys: https://www.danielgutierrez.com/sacred-journeys

In 2019 Daniel will embark on creating one of his

lifetime dreams to open his own center in the sacred valley of Peru. This center named after his late mother will be a place for his travels to stay and learn from Daniel's teachings and visit some of the most sacred sights in Peru. For more information: www.catalinacentrodeamor.com

LISTEN TO DANIEL'S SACRED JOURNEY RECORDINGS

Visit https://littleredrecorder.com to experience what happens when you combine Daniel's Sacred Journey field recordings with composer Adam King's atmospheric and orchestral compositions.

https://radiancemagazine.org/